PRAISE FOR

REMAKE THE WORLD

"Whenever I read Astra Taylor, I never want to stop. Affable and curious, she invites readers with her on a relentless exploration of the most crucial questions facing the left—and really, humanity—today. But don't let the congeniality fool you; Taylor is a radical working to remake our world. She writes for us, the ordinary and hungry public, searching for ideas that make sense of our desires for a better world. Rooted in rigorous study, deep questioning, and powerful and persuasive argument, Taylor's latest, *Remake the World*, is further evidence that she is the people's public intellectual."
—Keeanga-Yamahtta Taylor

"Astra Taylor has been remaking the world with her powerful thought and prophetic action for years. This wide-ranging book is a courageous and visionary embodiment of her deep commitment to fundamental transformation!" **—Cornel West**

"Astra Taylor's *Remake the World* is a valuable log of a militant's journey through our troubled times. Beautifully written in a warm, humorous, autobiographical style, it helps us think beyond the classic divisions in the left, while questioning whether anticapitalists can work within the state without compromising their political integrity and whether reform is always necessarily opposed to revolution. Whatever answer we give to these questions, this is a book we should read." **—Silvia Federici**

"Astra Taylor's crystalline writing is on full display in this collection of penetrating and profound essays, curated and necessary for these troubled times." **—Roxanne Dunbar-Ortiz**

"Astra Taylor is a rare public intellectual, utterly committed to asking humanity's most profound questions yet entirely devoid of pretensions and compulsively readable." **—Naomi Klein**

"One of the most incisive thinkers on participatory politics today." **—Molly Crabapple**

"Astra Taylor is both a deeply important thinker and a beautiful writer. She has the rare ability to make connections between subjects that desperately need to be seen as one. *Remake the World* brilliantly draws upon history to show us how to successfully challenge the present-day forces that have taken a battering ram to democracy. Taylor's work matters so much because she calls us to a bigger vision. Read this book, then take action." **—Jane McAlevey**

REMAKE THE WORLD

ESSAYS, REFLECTIONS, REBELLIONS

ASTRA TAYLOR

Haymarket Books
Chicago, Illinois

Published in 2021 by
Haymarket Books
P.O. Box 180165
Chicago, IL 60618
773-583-7884
www.haymarketbooks.org
info@haymarketbooks.org

ISBN: 978-1-64259-454-6

Distributed to the trade in the US through Consortium Book Sales
and Distribution (www.cbsd.com) and internationally through
Ingram Publisher Services International (www.ingramcontent.com).

This book was published with the generous support of Lannan
Foundation and Wallace Action Fund.

Special discounts are available for bulk purchases by organizations
and institutions. Please email orders@haymarketbooks.org for more
information.

Cover design by Tara Nye Taylor.

Library of Congress Cataloging-in-Publication data is available.

Entered into digital printing May, 2021.

For my father, Ethan Taylor,
who taught me to keep trying

CONTENTS

1

BREATHING TOGETHER

"It's as natural as breathing" is a cliché because, when all is going well, nothing else is more effortless than inhaling and exhaling, something we do approximately twenty thousand times a day. Typically, most of us don't think much about it. We breathe as we sleep, breathe as we eat, breathe as we move, and breathe as we talk. But that changed in 2020. We worried about our lungs and gasped for air. A novel illness sickened millions and tanked the global economy, thousands ingested tear gas protesting police violence, and cities were smothered by plumes of dark, noxious smoke from nearby forest fires.

During the first tense few weeks of the Covid-19 shutdown, we thought we could stop the spread of the disease by washing our hands. Our hands were something we could control. We could keep them in our pockets, wear latex gloves, have sanitizer at the ready, and scrub off the pathogen with soap and hot water. We didn't have all the facts. The coronavirus, as US authorities knew by early February, is airborne, transmitted through invisible particles and droplets emitted and ingested during the most automatic of physical acts. The pandemic has revealed "that our bodies function more like sponges than fortresses," my sister, the disability rights activist and scholar Sunaura Taylor, observed. "In a variety of visualizations, we see our bodies extending beyond their usual bounds: graphics of our coughs, sneezes, and even breath show how far beyond our own skin our bodies reach; the six-foot rule of social distancing a daily acknowledgement that our bodies not only leak and ooze, but that they absorb the conditions of others." Epidemiology and physics colluded to prove that even at a seemingly safe distance, we touch by virtue of breathing the same air.

In the worst cases, Covid-19 causes acute respiratory distress. Experts describe succumbing to the disease as akin to drowning. Early in the outbreak I read a piece by a doctor attempting to educate readers about how our lungs operate and what contracting the illness might entail. A healthy lung is so soft, she wrote, it "has almost no substance"; touching it feels like "reaching into a bowl of whipped cream." Covid changes that, filling the twin organs with a yellow goo that blocks the free flow of oxygen: "The lung texture changes, beginning to feel more like a marshmallow than whipped cream." To be soft and permeable like a sponge is to be healthy. To be rigid and closed off, fortresslike, spells doom. This is true, it turns out, not just for our lungs but also for our very selves.

When we breathe, we pull air into our windpipe, or trachea. That pipe than splits into our lungs' two main airways, called bronchi, which then branch off into smaller and smaller passageways, leading to tiny twig-like tubes called bronchioles that culminate in clusters of microscopic sacs called alveoli. In medical diagrams these passageways resemble the branches of an upside-down tree, as though every human being contains a piece of an inverted forest inside their chest. It's a fitting image, because if it weren't for trees, we wouldn't be able to breathe. By photosynthesizing, plants generate carbohydrates and oxygen in equal measure, nourishing our bellies and filling our lungs. Without them we'd starve, but not before we choked on lethal levels of carbon dioxide. In this sense, the thousands of fires that raged across North America in 2020, burning more than eight million acres, charred the lungs of the earth.

In those months, some communities gagged on smoke, others on pepper spray. On May 25, forty-six-year-old George Floyd was asphyxiated by Derek Chauvin, a Minneapolis police offer who kneeled on Floyd's neck for eight minutes and forty-six seconds with an expression of untouchable, detached superiority. Floyd's alleged transgression was using a counterfeit twenty-dollar bill. The assault was caught on video, and perhaps because the pandemic had slowed things down, people paid attention. Floyd's murder galvanized the biggest protest movement in US history, attracting up to twenty-six million participants by midsummer. Police and federal agents responded with unrelenting force, blinding over a dozen eyes with rubber bullets and burning thousands of people's lungs with chemical weapons, including smoke grenades. In Portland, Oregon, residents used leaf blowers for self-defense, redirecting fumes away from innocent crowds and back toward the cops. Floyd's last words echoed Eric Garner, who, as he was killed by police in New York City in 2014, uttered a phrase that would become a common chant at Black Lives Matter protests: "I can't breathe." In streets full of tear gas, demonstrators couldn't breathe either.

The right wing, predictably, responded to these developments with aggressive denial. Millions of people already devoted to conspiracy theories merely had to add a few new twists to preexisting narratives to bring them up to date. The coronavirus, like global warming, was a hoax, an elaborate ruse by an elite and evil cabal to control the populace—not a pandemic but a "plandemic." Likewise, the fires in California and Washington were not connected to shifting weather patterns caused by greenhouse gas emissions, but the result of arson, violent acts committed by mythic anarchists and anti-fascists who were never found but who were certainly in cahoots with Black Lives Matter. From his White House perch, Donald Trump amplified falsehoods, uplifted racists, and sowed confusion and doubt. Research showed he was the single largest source of disinformation about Covid-19. While condemning millions to disease and destitution, Trump told his followers they were victims not of a vastly unequal society (helmed by a sociopathic plutocrat no less) but of public health protocols and marginalized groups seeking equal rights. He comforted those afflicted with delusions that a reassertion of white supremacy and a revolt against a spectral "deep state" could cure the crisis. A network of right-wing individuals and foundations funded and fomented discontent, emboldening armed vigilantes who gathered at state capitols demanding a return to business as usual. In Michigan, the fourteen men arrested for plotting to kidnap Governor Gretchen Whitmer foreshadowed the throng that would enter the nation's Capitol on January 6, 2021, as Congress was certifying Joe Biden's electoral victory. Carrying weapons and plastic handcuffs, seemingly ready to take hostages, conservative fanatics overran security, denouncing traitors, waving Confederate flags, wearing neo-Nazi T-shirts, shouting racial slurs, and beating one Trump-supporting cop to death after he dared block their path. Instead of being snapped back to their senses by a fatal illness, people retreated further into fantasy and fallacy, in which face masks were part of a far-reaching conspiracy to suffocate patriots and stifle freedom.

According to my dictionary, a conspiracy is "a plotting of evil, unlawful design; a combination of persons for an evil purpose." This is the definition that describes the most popular conspiracy theories of our day, which claim to ferret out a demonic sect pulling society's strings, whether they are nefarious globalists, Jewish bankers, a Satanic pedophile ring, a "shadow government," or some dastardly combination thereof. While such misapprehensions are as old as the nation itself—some historians point out that the United States was born of a conspiracy theory, as evidenced by the Declaration of Independence's paranoid litany of Britain's "abuses and usurpations," including unleashing "merciless Indian savages" and "absolute despotism"—the Trump era was uniquely steeped in them. Trump's rise to power began with the racist lie of birtherism (insisting that Barack Obama was not a true US citizen) and ended in the authoritarian insistence that the election was rigged and stolen by "socialist" Democrats, with the help of some disloyal Republican officials (among them Attorney General William Barr and Vice President Mike Pence). While people on the political left are not immune to it, this kind of conspiracism is more endemic among and useful to the right wing.

If we go farther back, however, we'll find the word *conspiracy* has a different, more profound meaning that might help us comprehend our present predicament. It comes from the Latin *conspirationem*, "agreement, union, unanimity," and *conspirare*, "to be in agreement; to ally"—or, literally, "to breathe together." That is what the more powerful segment of society, the ruling class, have never wanted the rest of us to do—to come together as allies and, god forbid, form unions. Throughout US history, the most influential and destructive conspiracies have emanated not from the fringes but from the country's political and financial centers of power, and their goal has been preventing regular people from banding together to improve their lot. Economic elites have looted the public sphere while promoting an ideology of toxic individualism that has left people more isolated and susceptible to destructive, paranoid conspiracy theories that abet the right wing. We are all living amid the wreckage of a long, ongoing, and intentional sabotage of progressive collective action: a profit-driven health-care system ill-prepared to cope with a pandemic, runaway climate change threatening the future, a bigoted and broken criminal justice system, a misinformation-addled (and conspiracy-promoting) corporate media sphere, and an economy in which the majority of people can barely keep their heads above water. Our inability to truly conspire is why so many people are struggling to breathe today.

* * *

"The power to define what is and is not a conspiracy is a jealously guarded privilege," Michael Mark Cohen writes in his fascinating book *The Conspiracy of Capital: Law, Violence, and American Popular Radicalism in the Age of Monopoly*. In the early days of the United States, this battle would be fought overwhelmingly in the courts.

The first labor conspiracy case in the United States was the Philadelphia Cordwainers trial of 1805 to 1806, and it remains one of the most significant trials in labor history to this day. "A group of journeyman shoemakers attempted to combine to demand higher pay and prevent the hiring of replacement workers," Cohen explains, and in response they were charged with forming "a combination and conspiracy to raise wages." Shoemaking was one of the city's most profitable industries, and it was also the most contentious. A dispute over wages led to a seven-week strike and then a lawsuit, with eight journeymen indicted. A scab testified that the "workers were foreigners seeking to overthrow the laws of the United States" (the trope of the outside agitator was already in effect). The prosecution argued that the workers' collusion threatened not only the shoemaking industry but also the entire city's economy. While the workers got off with a small fine, the case set a disturbing precedent. Other courts interpreted the verdict as a ban on labor unions, which meant that organizing efforts were henceforth subject to suppression from both employers and the state. Between 1806 and 1842 there were more than twenty-one labor conspiracy trials involving "cordwainers, tailors, hatters, spinners, and carpet weavers," Cohen reports. Strikers won six of them. But in each and every case, unions were deemed illegal "combinations" and "conspiracies" and forbidden.

Speaking for countless others, Philadelphia labor leader Stephen Simpson railed against a double standard that tilted the playing field in favor of employers. "If mechanics combine to raise their wages, the laws punish them as conspirators against the good of society, and the dungeon awaits them as it does the robber," he wrote in 1831. "But the laws have made it a just and meritorious act, that capitalists shall combine to strip the man of labour of his earnings, and reduce him to a dry crust, and a gourd of water." Robert G. Ingersoll, a famed agnostic and social reformer, would later express the same sentiment in a pithier formulation: "If the rich meet to

reduce wages, that's a conference; if the poor resist the reduction, that's a conspiracy." The double standard would be
etched into law: at the same times workers were under attack,
the owning class was provided with a bevy of new rights. A
corporation would be redefined as a "legal person" entitled to
equal protection. Limited liability companies received state
sanction and support while labor unions were deemed illegal.

As the age of monopoly wore on, conspiracy charges ramped
up. The common law doctrine of criminal conspiracy allowed
the captains of industry to regulate working-class organization
with incessant litigation, turning courtrooms into centers of
class conflict. A vague and broad accusation, the conspiracy
doctrine implied guilt by association and was used to suppress
dissent, "to ban unions, outlaw strikes, pickets, and boycotts,
to criminalize radical ideologies like anarchism and communism," in Cohen's words. The doctrine was considered "the
darling of the prosecutor's nursery" for its sweeping application and loose evidentiary rules, which meant it was perfect for
suppressing dissent—anyone could be sucked into the ring of
conspirators, even those who had never met before. "If there
are still any citizens interested in protecting human liberty, let
them study the conspiracy laws of the United States," the re-
nowned radical lawyer Clarence Darrow, implored. "No one's
liberty is safe."

Born in 1857, Darrow defended countless workers and organizers from conspiracy charges over his career, inspired, in
part, by the famous Haymarket trial, a miscarriage of justice
that saw eight anarchists charged with conspiracy and seven
sentenced to death for an explosion at a small rally (a pardon
would be issued in time to save three of them). In an attempt to
mount more successful defenses, Darrow dug into the conspir-

acy doctrine's history to uncover its basis in English common law, only to discover that its original purpose had been turned on its head. First codified in 1305, the conspiracy doctrine began as a medieval rule designed to prevent malicious persecution. "It was an ancient law that a man who conspired to use the courts to destroy his fellow-men was guilty of treason to the state," Darrow concluded. "He had laid his hand upon the State itself; he had touched the bulwark of human liberty."

The Age of Revolution flipped the script, shifting the doctrine's purpose from the prevention and punishment of private abuse of the jury system to the subversion of efforts to build working-class solidarity. In 1721, English judges ruled in *Rex v. Journeymen Tailors of Cambridge* that workers' efforts to strike to raise wages amounted to an unlawful and criminal conspiracy, setting the stage for the Combination Acts of 1799 and 1800, which made trade unionism illegal in Britain, though laborers continued to put up fierce resistance. "The aristocracy were interested in repressing the Jacobin 'conspiracies' of the people," Cohen explains, while "the manufacturers were interested in defeating their 'conspiracies to increase wages.'" The Combination Acts did both. A cross section of elites gained power, and labor was forced into the shadows. As a result, the historian E. P. Thompson notes in his study of the English working class, organizing became more furtive, or "conspiratorial" in its modern-day sense. Workers could unite only in secret, ever watchful for employers, magistrates, parsons, and spies who might be their undoing.

Workers fought back, but always from a defensive crouch. In the United States, laborers exploited on the job faced retaliation for demanding better treatment. They could be fired, wounded, or lynched, whether by hired Pinkerton guards or volunteer reactionary mobs. World War I inflamed ethno-nationalist tensions and put targets on the backs of radicals, with thousands arrested and often deported in the infamous Palmer Raids. The wartime Espionage Act strengthened the hand of the state, making it possible to prosecute labor partisans for words alone. The legendary organizer Eugene Debs was jailed for declaring that the only war in which he would enlist "was the war of the workers of the world against the exploiters of the world." Voicing that sentiment landed him in prison for sedition, a charge held up by a unanimous Supreme Court decision.

With hindsight, we regard the Haymarket affair, the first wave of the Red Scare, and the Palmer Raids as egregious abuses of state power. But rather than being aberrations, they epitomize a troubling current that has coursed through US history since the colonial period, carried across the Atlantic via British common law all the way to the present—a disastrous determination to squelch the efforts of working people to become organized. "The most dangerous conspiracy theories, especially rightwing conspiracy theories, do not exclusively populate the extremist margins of American politics and history," Cohen observes. "Rather, the most dangerous conspiracy theories in American politics emerge from the very center of power, in which white supremacist, anticommunist, and anti-terrorist ideologies, each defined by shifting fears of subversive conspiracies, are promoted and enacted by presidents, business leaders, military men, judges, prosecutors, police, and vigilantes." In other words, the most destructive purveyors of conspiracy theories are not average people who anxiously embrace half-truths. Rather, the real threat comes from those who hold official positions of influence and who cynically trade in damaging lies to maintain dominance, fully aware that their continued authority depends on the disorientation, distraction, demoralization, and disarray of millions of others. If that sounds conspiratorial, it is. "I think a little conspiratorialism on the left is sometimes healthy. There actually is a cabal of ruling elites that seek to poison and imprison this world in the name of profits," Cohen told me by email. "And those people have names, addresses and regularly meet to plot their crimes against humanity and nature. We have much to gain by naming and fighting them both individually and as a group."

* * *

In 1961, sociologist Daniel Bell speculated that there is "in the American temper, a feeling that 'somewhere,' 'somebody' is pulling all the complicated strings to which this *jumbled world dances.*" The esteemed historian Richard Hofstadter echoed that sentiment, publishing *The Paranoid Style in American Politics* to great acclaim. Over the course of the Trump presidency, countless op-eds, journalistic exposés, academic articles, and books have articulated a similar concern, citing the explosion of conspiracy theories and the elevation of some of the most outlandish ones to the halls of power. The same election that evicted Trump from the White House secured victory for two congressional candidates who publicly supported QAnon, a convoluted conspiracy devoted to interpreting message board missives from "Q," a mysterious figure and supposed government insider with knowledge of Trump's plan to vanquish the Devil-worshiping, child-molesting globalists who currently run the world and send them to Guantánamo Bay with the help of John F. Kennedy Jr., who faked his own death in 1999 and has been in hiding ever since. At the end of 2020, NPR and Ipsos published the results of a poll assessing QAnon's reach. Seventeen percent of respondents said it was "true" that "a group of Satan-worshipping elites who run a child sex ring are trying to control our politics and media," and 37 percent more said they didn't know. Without a doubt, it is alarming when millions of people reject basic reality, clinging to the bizarre conviction that an established serial sexual harasser of women and cager of real children at the border is actually the savior of illusory abused youngsters. Yet attempts to diagnose the problem's source and identify possible cures too often fall short.

The book *A Lot of People Are Saying*, from 2019, epitomizes the genre. Authors Nancy Rosenblum and Russell Muirhead describe what they call the "new conspiracism," or "conspiracy without theory." In their schema, classic conspiracism's evidentiary basis (picture dozens of JFK assassination aficionados poring over photographs of the grassy knoll) has been abandoned in favor of pure affect; hypotheses and suppositions gain purchase through repetition, not proof. Digital networks drown internet users in dubious information designed less to persuade than to overwhelm, as social media users circulate and recirculate sensational claims. Those who know how to game algorithms amass enormous followings, and those with the most "engaging" content always win, accuracy be damned.

In 2020, millions of jobs evaporated overnight, but hucksters hit pay dirt. The clickbait economy launched the careers of an astonishing number of "conspiracy entrepreneurs," a handful of whom, like Alex Jones, are national figures while the vast majority carve out an obscure niche, perhaps exposing "crisis actors" (the people who purportedly pretend to be victims of mass shootings as part of a larger plot to undermine the Second Amendment) or tracking "chem trails" (mind-controlling vapors allegedly released by planes). Rosenblum and Muirhead quote Stefanie MacWilliams, a twentysomething woman from Belleville, Ontario, who gained notoriety for propagating the myth of "Pizzagate," which held that prominent Democratic political operatives (including Hillary Clinton and John Podesta) ran a pedophile ring housed at a popular pizza parlor in Washington, DC, called Comet Ping Pong. This inspired a man to travel from North Carolina, enter the premises, and fire a military assault rifle, demanding the release of imaginary sex slaves he believed were being held in a nonexistent basement. Despite the fact that someone could have been killed during the commotion, MacWilliams was unremorseful: "I really have no regrets and it's honestly really grown our audience."

A Lot of People Are Saying maintains that while conspiracism has long pervaded US politics, something significant has changed in recent years. "Today, conspiracism is not, as we might expect, the last resort of permanent political losers, but the first resort of winners," the authors observe, in a reference to Donald Trump's rule as conspiracist-in-chief and the Republican Party's tendency to paint itself as a victim even as it wields political power. For all the authors' supposed historical acuity, their insistence that conspiracy theories originating from the powerful is a *new* phenomenon only holds if you selectively interpret and idealize the past. A cursory glance at US history, or a close read of Michael Mark Cohen, shows that the powerful have claimed to be victims since the founding of the nation. The lies peddled by Trump and the Grand Old Party are just the latest iterations of the truth-destroying, state-building ideologies of yore.

Today we use the term Red Scare to indicate an overreaction, but the mania lasted the better part of the twentieth century, peaking twice, first around World War I and then after World War II. During the second surge, the House Un-American Activities Committee (HUAC) devoted incredible energy to pinpointing communist influence in government and industry, an influence that zealots detected in New Deal social programs, strong labor protections and trade union militancy, and the civil rights movement, which Representative John Rankin of Mississippi denounced as "communistic bunk." Operating in a similar vein, Senator Joseph McCarthy launched a crusade in Congress, seeking out subversive elements in Washington and Hollywood. His efforts lost steam only when they were broadcast on national television and public opinion turned against his inquisition. (It's worth noting that McCarthy's mercenary and underhanded chief counsel, Roy Cohn, went on to become one of Trump's best friends and mentors). But of course, the conspiracism didn't stop with the end of the warped government hearings. Under the fervid anticommunist leadership of J. Edgar Hoover, the Federal Bureau of Investigation continued to spy on citizens, including via COINTELPRO, a counterintelligence program designed to surveil, infiltrate, discredit, and disrupt left-wing groups. As one official memo put it, the aim was to "enhance the paranoia endemic in [dissident] circles" and convince activists that FBI agents lurked "behind every mailbox." A letter sent by the program tried to pressure Martin Luther King Jr. to kill himself. The CIA abetted the cause with Operation CHAOS, initiated by President Lyndon Johnson in 1967 and expanded by Richard Nixon, which "infiltrated antiwar groups, black power organizations, and even women's consciousness raising sessions to determine if foreign communists were secretly directing them."

As Kathryn Olmsted documents in her illuminating book *Real Enemies*, US citizens are suspicious of their government for good reason. Government lies have cost livelihoods and lives. In 1962, the Joint Chiefs of Staff presented Secretary of Defense Robert McNamara with a plan to deceive Americans into supporting a war on Cuba by launching self-inflicted terror attacks on US soil. While that idea was scuttled, US policies of duplicity and violence were par for the course in Vietnam, Cambodia, Argentina, Guatemala, Indonesia, and elsewhere. In its final tally, anticommunism is responsible for the deaths of millions of people worldwide.

As these and many other abuses of power were revealed, the public became increasingly perturbed. After HUAC, McCarthyism, Watergate, COINTELPRO, and the Iran–Contra scandal, anything seemed possible, and many assumed more explosive secrets must lie in store. September 11, 2001, appeared to validate their gravest fears. The George W. Bush administration made an unprecedented grab of executive authority to battle a nebulous enemy and cooked up a baseless story about weapons of mass destruction to deceive the public into supporting war with Iraq. Brown University's Watson Institute estimates that over five hundred thousand people have perished as a result of the war on terror, not counting casualties in Syria. As if deception and carnage weren't bad enough, a movement of 9/11 "Truthers" are convinced something even more diabolical transpired—the destruction of the World Trade Center towers was an "inside job." There was no limit, some believed, to what the government might do. Bush-era conspiracy theorists, Olmsted notes, were "more interested in making accusations and identifying the government as irredeemably evil than enacting reforms." The same holds for millions of suspicious minds today.

"The new conspiracism drains the sense that democratic government is legitimate without supplying any alternative standards," Rosenblum and Muirhead write in *A Lot of People Are Saying*. They're correct, but we have to understand the cause. For the last century, anticommunism run amok helped repress legitimate and necessary alternatives, leaving nihilistic reaction and unhinged conjecture to fill the void.

* * *

Eight months into the pandemic, a television news station in Kalamazoo, Michigan, broadcast a telling exchange. The newscaster stood in a desolate suburban parking lot, reporting on the reaction to the state's new Covid-19 restrictions. The owner of a nearby establishment, a weary-looking older man, walked up and told the host he had something to say. He was resisting the shutdown and wanted to say why.

"My government leaders have abandoned me," he said. "They've put me in a position where I have to fight back." Four trillion dollars of stimulus money was given to special-interest groups and campaign donors, he continued, "enough money to give every family, *every family in this country*, $20,000 to go home for two months." If he were given that sort of support, the man said, he gladly would have closed shop and let the virus settle down. "But I'm not going to do it alone." When asked if he would continue to violate the state order, the man was defiant. "This isn't a state order; this is a conspiracy, a tyranny . . . and I've got patriots coming out and supporting me." The eighty-second clip encapsulated the ways government failures fuel conspiratorial thinking. On one level, the man was correct and his indignation justified. When the bailout funds were dispersed in the spring of 2020, a conspiracy of sorts was indeed afoot—bankers and corporate executives made a mad grab for public money with few strings attached, while regular people, who should have been paid to stay home, scraped by on crumbs. But he was wrong to imagine patriotism and a reckless disregard for public health as the solution to a problem caused by plutocracy. After all, the rich can share citizenship status with poor and working people and still dispossess them.

Numerous studies show that insecure, vulnerable, and threatened populations are more susceptible to conspiracism. "Conspiratorial ideation" is driven by both ideology and instability. Feelings of powerlessness, research shows, predict such beliefs. In *Republic of Lies*, Anna Merlan cites an analysis of letters by readers of the *New York Times* and *Chicago Tribune* between 1890 and 2010 that found that conspiracy theories fluctuated in response to times of enormous social upheaval, with the first spike around 1900. Research also indicates that conspiracy beliefs are high particularly among members of stigmatized minority groups. But as Merlan rightly points out, these groups have well-founded grounds for mistrust, given the violent history of white supremacy in this country. Not every community's sense of persecution is equally valid, and an awareness of persecution doesn't always yield antisocial attitudes. Unlike individuals awash in white resentment, Black people do not tend to be reactionary zealots, despite ample reasons to be skeptical of the state and its racist double standards.

In a society as unequal and unsupportive as ours, masses of people aren't wrong to feel beleaguered. The tragedy—and farce—is that the popular explanations for the causes of their suffering, and the potential antidotes they reach for are often poisonous. In a perverse way, many prominent conspiracy theories are a cry for justice and connection, even if they frame the world in a Manichaean binary of good versus evil, shunning a structural analysis along with complexity and contingency—positing a cadre of cartoon villains who possess the incredible ability to mastermind world events, leaving nothing to chance. Nevertheless, such theories are typically populist in form, in that they purport to expose the destructive actions of a power elite against regular, unwitting people (a power elite sadly often imagined in ways shot through with anti-Semitism). QAnon's slogan "Where we go one, we go all," often shortened to #WWG1WGA, evokes the Wobbly motto "An injury to one is an injury to all," by way of the Three Musketeers. It's a mash-up of cultural references, stereotypes, thwarted expectations, and twisted idealism. Some of those who "stormed" the Capitol in early 2021 appeared to genuinely believe they were on a mission to stop a crime of epic proportions, including a massive human trafficking ring and the suppression of millions of votes (a "sacred landslide election victory," in Trump's fantasy). The real perpetrators, however, are the people who know better, including senators Ted Cruz and Josh Hawley, graduates of Harvard Law School and Yale Law School, respectively, and more than one hundred Republican House members who wittingly conned the crowd, encouraging them before and after the failed siege.

The horrifying actions of January 6 and the storming of various state capitols make clear that many conspiracists are irredeemable racists and authentic fascists who must not be placated or pandered to. But there are undoubtedly some who might be receptive to other messages—including the basic insight that ruling elites seek to maintain dominance by a strategy to deceive, divide, and conquer—if they were as omnipresent and aggressively promoted. We'll never know how many people would prefer the opportunity to have a face-to-face conversation with a community organizer instead of watching a talking head spout nonsense online, because they never get such a knock on the door and a chance to connect. Far from the country of civic associations described by Alexis de Tocqueville in *Democracy in America*, the US today is a land of anomie where, sociologists observe, a growing number of people suffer from an "epidemic of loneliness." Huge numbers of people in the United States report having no close friends. Even fewer have comrades.

The spread of misinformation and fake news has inspired hand-wringing among liberals, who bemoan the public's gullibility and lack of knowledge. I confess I've wrung my hands, too. But it's not enough to denounce fake news or bewail the inability of regular readers to verify facts or "trust science" (a telling phrase since "trust" is unthinking, an act of faith rather than critical reflection—it means, in effect, know your place). Of course, some people could use a look in the mirror—many liberals spent the Trump years deeply invested in "Russiagate," which played into dated, xenophobic Cold War clichés about "the Russians" and exaggerated foreign influence while failing to acknowledge homegrown threats to democracy. After all, it was the Electoral College that handed Trump the presidency, not Vladimir Putin. Worse still, liberals came to lionize the very institutions—the FBI and CIA—that have been the primary agents of countersubversive conspiracies, trampling liberties and destroying lives around the world.

As Jonathan Swift quipped in 1721, "Reasoning will never make a Man correct an ill Opinion, which by Reasoning he never acquired." Ideologies are always shaped by emotions and informed by lived experience. The man in Kalamazoo represents millions who are justifiably angry because they have indeed been abandoned, and who are desperately grasping for explanations that make sense of their circumstances. The challenge is reaching them before mendacious narratives do. But given corporate America's long and effective assault on labor unions, quality free public education, and nonprofit media—the means and channels through which understanding generally spread—that is increasingly difficult. Twitter, Facebook, Apple, and Google's attempts to diminish the digital presence of the far right in the waning days of the Trump presidency—including terminating Trump's personal accounts—were too little, too late.

The bipartisan project of undermining the left in this country has been, quite literally, a fool's errand. By destroying the social solidarity, economic equality, and class-conscious worldview that a robust, organized left helps provide, ruling elites have created a vacuum in which unhinged conspiracies propagate. Far from being a rational system as proponents claim, capitalism ineluctably tends toward the illogical and ludicrous. Plutocrats will embrace and promote paranoia as long it is profitable; manufactured lunacy provides useful cover, distracting the public from unpopular policies (tax cuts, attacks on unions, a decimated safety net), just as obsessively naming enemies (Democrats, the press, communists, socialists, antifa, anarchists, feminists, intellectuals, "woke" students, and so on) deflects responsibility and blame. In the memorable words of Stephen Bannon, conservatives counteract the allegedly liberal media by "flood[ing] the zone with shit." The goal is not to manufacture consent but to promulgate confusion, and digital capitalism expands the arsenal used to assault our senses. (In 2020, videos endorsing false claims of widespread voter fraud were viewed on YouTube more than 138 million times during the week of the election alone; polls soon showed that one-third of Americans believed that voter fraud helped Joe Biden win.) "Those who persistently blame others for indulging in conspiracies have a strong tendency to engage in plots themselves," Theodor Adorno smartly observed in 1952, and so it goes today.

The world is a complicated place, and we are permeable, interconnected beings subject to infection by ideas and viruses. We are connected across time and space: our beliefs shaped by past events, our bodies impacted by what happens on the other side of the planet, our lungs filled with air exhaled in the next room. Autonomy is an impossibility. Faced with the prospect of this revelation, some recoil, taking solace in revanchist notions of separation, nationalism, and self-reliance laced with magical thinking. Given the fact of interconnection, the rest of us will never be able to wholly isolate ourselves from these individuals, however much we might like to. Instead, we have to work to combat and transform the ideologies, institutions, and incentives that enable and embolden them.

To have a chance of bringing people back to reality, or preventing them from losing touch in the first place, we will need to speak to their apprehensions and misgivings. Consider the growing suspicion of vaccines, which correlates with religious affiliation and higher socioeconomic status, making it one of the preferred conspiracy theories of the comparatively privileged. While anti-vaxxers are a serious threat to public health, there are plenty of reasons to be wary of the medical and pharmaceutical industries. Bill Gates using vaccinations to microchip the masses is not one of them. Or take speculation about the source of Covid-19. The fact is, viruses don't care about the imaginary boundaries human beings construct, whether those are national borders or the species barrier. Like other zoonotic diseases, the coronavirus jumped from one creature (likely a bat or pangolin) to our kind. It did so because industrial patterns of land use and meat production—picture clear-cut forests, crowded factory farms, and so-called wet markets—push human and nonhuman animals into ever-more intimate contact. In other words, while Covid-19 was not concocted in a Chinese lab or caused by 5G wireless towers, as cranks insist, it has political dimensions worth unraveling and discussing, particularly if we want to prevent the next deadly pandemic.

An ancient habit of the human mind, conspiracism will never be entirely stamped out, but it can be diminished if we deprive it of the instability, inequality, and isolation on which it feeds. "We will not be a less paranoid country until we are a fairer one," Merlan correctly observes. You can't fact-check people out of a problem that requires collective action, mass empowerment, and clearheaded strategy to solve. Instead of chastisement we need a credible vision of a better society and a recognition that it will take mass movements to manifest it. That means building the one thing nostalgic right-wingers and neoliberal centrists both hate to see—an organized and mobilized multiracial working class fighting for their shared interests. It will take a conspiracy of epic proportions to counteract this country's ruinous and unrelenting war on people's ability to come together for the common good, but that's the only way we'll all ever be able to breathe.

2

FAILING BETTER

I have a drawer where I keep records of many projects that, for some reason or another, hit a wall—a container of failures. There are proposals for films, notes for unwritten manifestos, and blueprints of political crusades my comrades and I don't have the time or money to pursue. But there's one project that's a bigger flop than all the others: the manuscript of a nonfiction book that I researched and wrote, on and off, for five years. The book is about the conflicted political legacy of the sixties for people who grew up in the decade's aftermath, and for many years I felt terrible that I couldn't pull it together.

As a child of the counterculture (third generation—my grandmother, who lived in Toronto at the time, was on the hippie vanguard), I was interested in the way my experience defied the mainstream expectation that I would rebel against my parents and become a Republican or Conservative, like the kid in the sitcom I never saw because we didn't watch television. I was also interested in how the sixties cast a shadow

---

* Previously published as "From the Ashes of Occupy: On Failing Better and Erasing Debts," *Hazlitt*, November 14, 2013.

over all subsequent political activities, serving as both inhibitor and inspiration. The decade was simultaneously extolled as a pinnacle of protest, one we in the present could never live up to, and dismissed as a risible relic, sometimes in the same breath. I was fascinated by our society's conflicted relationship to the time and all the currents it contained: the history of the civil rights, feminist, and antiwar movements, the communes and alternative schools that were started by the thousands, and the right-wing backlash triggered by all this. Then there were the veterans of the period I interviewed, who could be both sanctimonious and contrite, proud and full of regret.

I wasn't trying to present the correct view of one of the most written about and debated decades—that would have been folly. Rather, I was interested in ambiguity and how the meaning of events could change over time. Again and again I returned to the theme of failure, wondering how it was defined. If a commune lasted a few years or even a decade, was it a failure or a short-lived success? If the experience of planning an anticlimactic demonstration motivated someone to develop new effective organizing tactics, should the demonstration be counted as a defeat or a victory? How, I wondered, do we define what's futile and what's worthwhile, what has an impact and what doesn't?

* * *

When Occupy Wall Street started in September 2011 and I found myself in Zuccotti Park day after day, unable to resist the bizarre and growing gathering of the discontented, my friends would ask me if I was making a documentary about it. I would explain that I didn't want to watch things unfold at a remove, that somehow the idea of making a film about

Occupy's rise and decline made me sad. I knew the decline would inevitably come. Instead, I felt an obligation to try to push the movement along and extend its reach, to paddle against the current with everyone else, not just stand on the sidelines holding a camera, watching others sweat.

It wasn't until well after the occupation ended, though, that I found a way in—crossing the line from supportive observer to obsessive organizer by joining forces with a burgeoning coalition dedicated to exploring the possibilities of debt resistance. To talk to people during the first few weeks of Occupy Wall Street was to talk about student loans that couldn't be repaid, medical bills that were piling up, houses that had been reclaimed by bailed-out banks, and insolvent communities forced to endure austerity measures. Debt bridges the personal and political, binding individuals to a broader set of economic circumstances, and as such presents a powerful opportunity to unite otherwise divided populations. Maybe debt was something we could work with?

When I was writing my book about the sixties I speculated that student debt was one of the reasons why so few young people were in the streets protesting the wars in Iraq and Afghanistan—they were too busy trying to make money for their monthly payments. That's the trap I was in at the time. I saw debt was an effective means of social control, one with roots that reach back to Ronald Reagan's grudge against student protesters when he was California's governor in the sixties. The emergence of Occupy was a welcome sign that the control mechanism was breaking down. Rising debt loads and the slumping economy were combining to cause young people to doubt they would ever be able to pay off the unfair or odious debts around their necks. Refusing those debts and demanding a new arrangement was beginning to seem like a legitimate option.

* * *

In late 2012 we launched an initiative called the Rolling Jubilee, a mechanism to purchase and erase people's past-due debts. Our ambitions were relatively modest. We aimed to raise $50,000 through a telethon hosted at a venue in lower Manhattan, and livestreamed to anyone who cared to watch. With that money we estimated we could buy and abolish $1 million of medical debt, while highlighting the injustice of a system that drives millions of sick people and their families into bankruptcy, and in which misfortune can be bought and sold. A portfolio of medical debt is a portfolio of misery.

The telethon planning committee—me, filmmaker Laura Hanna, music critic Michael Azerrad, and master of ceremonies David Rees—roped in sympathetic friends to provide entertainment, mixing speed lectures on inequality, stand-up comedy, a duet by my partner Jeff Mangum and Fugazi's Guy Picciotto, and performances by TV on the Radio and an all-lady mariachi band. It was an edifying and unpredictable night, but the telethon was almost redundant. A Tumblr post by an actor who had appeared on *Star Trek: The Next Generation* helped make the campaign go viral and we exceeded our fundraising goal before the first act even took to the stage.

By the end of the night we had raised almost $600,000. In the process, a small number of us had committed ourselves to being full-time volunteer debt abolishers, perhaps the first of our kind in the history of the world. Endless meetings with legal experts, accounting professionals, and moles in the debt industry would soon follow. We had to master a field that was alien to us and that we were explicitly hostile to. The Rolling Jubilee was a risky undertaking for many reasons, and were it not for the tireless effort of the core team—the countless conference calls, the mornings spent poring over documents and contracts—it could have been a disaster. That we have done what we said we were going to do, honoring our donors and spending their money as wisely as we could, is a tremendous relief. That we have already heard back from some of the people whose debts have been abolished makes all the anxiety and exertion seem worthwhile. The debtors got letters in the mail, and responded with gratitude, shock, and disbelief. Some have a hard time believing that the Rolling Jubilee is not a scam, since it sounds too good to be true.

* * *

Participating in Occupy in any capacity, even being part of the Rolling Jubilee, has never been easy for me. In many ways it goes against the fundamental currents of my personality. I, for one, would rather read about history than make it, since real political work involves continuous interpersonal negotiations, meetings that never end, and receiving and responding to hundreds of emails a day. It's reactive, not contemplative, and I prefer life with more of the latter. There's a myth that activism is the natural domain of a certain subset of human beings that thrive in group discussions, protest planning sessions, and vegan potlucks. I'm just "not that type"—people who otherwise identify as leftists demur, when asked why they stick to the realm of theory as opposed to action. It's a myth that lets us off the hook, perpetuating the old idea that it's someone else's calling to actually make change, though it's a mantle that falls to particular groups over time: the proletariat, the poor, the oppressed, the students, the people of color, the activist types, the not-us.

Sometimes I still think I'm "not that type" and want to quit and spend my time on other things. Let the born activists go out and plan protests; I want to stay in and read, analyze, debate, and pass judgment. That's where I'm most comfortable. It's a division of labor that appeals to me, even if I oppose it philosophically. For one, it's distorting. To outsiders, it's easy to prescribe methods and measures to activists: unions, for example, should appeal to people beyond their membership and build common cause; environmentalists should lobby the government to invest in green energy; Occupy should have pushed for full employment; and so on. But these maps are only truly legible from afar: as soon as you zoom in and try to figure out how to actually get from point A to point B things get murky, the path forward covered in brush, and the horizon impossible to discern. The map one can draw at a distance lacks the detail needed to actually follow it on the ground, which doesn't mean it's not worth drawing. What it means is that we need more people who can switch back and forth between the macro and micro view, who understand the challenges and obstacles that emerge when you are in the thick of things.

To do this means becoming more acquainted with failure, something most of us would rather avoid. Like those who prefer punditry to campaigning, I like to be right. And messy political work doesn't always allow for the certainty that opining does. Even if you're the self-righteous sort—a tendency I confess to sharing with many activists—wanting to be right is something different, a vice common to the intellectuals and professional prattlers. If you care about being smart and having an analysis that trumps the others, it's safer to be cynical about attempts to create social change, and to list all the logical reasons such efforts will likely fail—to always bet on the status quo maintaining its grip. Activism requires a kind of willed hopefulness, a readiness to bash your head against a wall so that it may crumble or crack, even if you know all the arguments about why what you're doing is probably doomed and all the reasons the wall is unlikely to budge.

* * *

The Rolling Jubilee can seem too good to be true, but at the same time it is not nearly enough (something our critics on the left never tired of reminding us). It will not, on its own, end the debt cycle or overthrow capitalism. The Rolling Jubilee was always meant as a spark, not a solution. We know we can't abolish all the medical debt, let alone all the other kinds of debt, held by US citizens. The total amount of debt we initially bought and abolished—over $30 million—is a drop in the ocean, sloshing around an America in arrears. And we know that even if we could make all this debt dissolve overnight, the underlying dynamic that puts people into such a state would remain unchanged, and that they would just start moving steadily back into the red.

Given this, those of us who spearheaded the Rolling Jubilee never saw the campaign as an end in itself. Instead we hoped it might serve as a stepping-stone to a debt resistance movement, to concerted collective action against economic exploitation, peonage, and endless tribute to the creditor class. What we ultimately need is a jubilee—a cancellation of debts—coupled with a profound economic transformation that addresses the underlying causes and conditions. In the United States things like universal health care, free public education, truly livable wages so people can stop going into debt to pay for basic needs, and new forms of socially productive credit that don't tie people in chains of compound interest would go a long way toward this end.

* * *

I just drew a map from on high, one that advises we go from A to B without suggesting any specific routes that will help us make the journey. A jubilee and an economic transformation sound divine, but it's a big demand against which formidable and amply funded forces are aligned. How will we find a way forward? Where can you go to learn how power works and how to organize against it? Lessons in strategic tenacity, in failing again and failing better, aren't on any curriculum I've ever seen, though they should be. Political organizing is a skill that precious few institutions exist to pass on. Instead we leave each new generation to reinvent the wheel given the limited tools and historical knowledge they have at hand, and roll our eyes when it flies out from under them.

My book on the sixties was a failure, but in retrospect a fruitful one. As a result of working on it, I approached Occupy with more patience than I might have otherwise, well aware that bygone social movements are bathed in a nostalgic light that obscures all the doubt, confusion, and sensations of impotence that attended them. I was more aware of the fact that seeds planted often take many years to grow, that they can be scattered to unexpected places and lie dormant for long spells only to suddenly sprout and flourish. I saw flaws too, like the era's dependence on charismatic leaders and the destructive generational divide, which sabotaged solidarity across age groups by insisting young people were the true agents of social change when there's no way they can fix everything alone.

The fact is, when it comes to changing the world, no one really knows what will work, though some have better instincts than others and are less afraid to follow them. My comrades and I have kept experimenting, each step yielding insights. Some ideas turn out to be dead ends and others open up new avenues and possibilities. The Rolling Jubilee inspired some of us to hatch plans to found the Debt Collective, a debtors' union dedicated to aggregating and harnessing its members' collective economic power. The Rolling Jubilee thus continued to roll on, evolving into a new form that has provided mutual aid, political education, and debt relief to tens of thousands of people in arrears. No doubt, some of our future schemes may find their final resting place in a drawer of failures, but I've come to the conclusion that that isn't necessarily such a terrible fate.

3

AGAINST ACTIVISM

B ack in 2006 I attended a conference called "1968" at a nondescript college in New Jersey. Mark Rudd, a student radical turned community college math instructor living out his retirement in New Mexico, delivered the keynote. Taking the podium, he reflected critically on the national renown he had earned in his early twenties for his role in the Columbia University occupation and his involvement with the Weather Underground, a mediagenic group of militant rebels who preached the gospel of "propaganda of the deed" by detonating bombs in places like the Pentagon and the Capitol. (As for violence against people, the group was ultimately responsible for inadvertently killing or wounding only their own comrades.) The audience members, mostly graduate students and twentysomething politicos like myself, were disposed to cheer Rudd's revolutionary past, impressed by the years he spent living as a fugitive. The Weathermen may have crossed a line and not really accomplished much, we reasoned, but at least they *took action*!

---

* Previously published as "Against Activism," *Baffler*, no. 30 (March 2016).

Rudd challenged our easy romanticism. Unlike many of his peers, who had become more conservative with age, Rudd remained committed to the political ideals that had guided him in his youth. But he had wholly reassessed the confrontational tactics on which he had built his reputation. The macho bluster, the calls to "pick up the gun"—those, he saw now, had been based in delusion. Fancying themselves a privileged group of revolutionary agents destined to catalyze a "white fighting force" to "aid the people of the world," he and his comrades had succeeded only in diminishing a base that had been painstakingly built up over years. "The FBI should have put us on the payroll," he said.

What he had failed to grasp back in the day, Rudd explained, patiently crushing our insurrectionary fantasies, was the difference between activism and organizing, between self-expression and movement building. It's a message he is still spreading. "The only time I heard the term *activist* fifty years ago was as part of an epithet used against student organizers by our official enemies, university administrators and newspaper editorialists," Rudd told me. "Mindless activists" was the phrase, and Rudd wonders now, half-jokingly, if "mindless" and "activist" don't somehow go together. At Columbia, he developed a rhetorical position he would repeat to anyone who would listen: "Organizing is another word for going slow." But lately he prefers Joe Hill's oft-quoted 1915 telegram to Bill Haywood: "Don't waste any time mourning, organize!" As it happens, 1915 was around the same year the word *activist* first appeared—so in a way, that's when the mourning really began.

* * *

Unlike the term *organizer*, with its clear roots in trade union and labor politics, *activist* has murky origins. According to the *Oxford English Dictionary*, the word has been quietly biding its time for over a century. Associated early on with German idealist philosopher Rudolf Eucken—who believed that striving is necessary to a spiritual life—it was then sometimes used to describe outspoken supporters of the Central Powers during the First World War. Eventually, the term came to signify political action more broadly, and though the precise path of this transformation remains to be traced by scholars more diligent than myself, it is clear that *activism* and *activist* have been in circulation with their current meanings for some time. In the early 1960s the *New York Times* described both Bertrand Russell and C. Wright Mills as activists (Mills's editor objected to the characterization in an angry letter), and searches through archival records from that period reveal scattered mentions of labor activists, and then civil rights activists, and then student activists.

"We used to call ourselves, variously, revolutionaries, radicals, militants, socialists, communists, organizers," Roxanne Dunbar-Ortiz, a radical historian with fifty years of social movement experience, told me. The rise of the word *activist*, she speculated, corresponds with what she describes as a broader "discrediting of the left." A good number of Rudd's and Dunbar-Ortiz's politically active peers came from dedicated communist or labor families, or had joined the fight for civil rights in the South, which meant they had firsthand knowledge of a movement deeply rooted in churches and community organizations, many of which employed (poorly) paid field organizers to mobilize people over sustained periods of time and against long odds.

It was only after the 1960s ended, as new social movements erupted—feminism, gay liberation, environmentalism, and disability rights—that activists truly began to proliferate. By the eighties and nineties, the term was firmly in common usage. These social movements accomplished a tremendous amount in a remarkably short time frame, often by building on and adapting long-standing organizing techniques while also inventing open, democratic, and nonhierarchical procedures. Yet in their quest to jettison some of the left's baggage, potentially useful frameworks, traditions, and methods were also cast aside.

Activists flourished as people moved away from what they felt were dated political ideologies—the anti-imperialist Marxism-Leninism that captivated the Weathermen went out of vogue, as the Communist Party had before it—and embraced emerging radical identities. In the wake of the sixties, people also, understandably, wanted to be less beholden to charismatic leadership, which put movements at risk of being sabotaged when figureheads were assassinated (Martin Luther King Jr.), acted unaccountably (Eldridge Cleaver), or switched sides (Jerry Rubin). Over the years, as unions lost their edge and became overrun by cautious or corrupt bureaucrats, cynicism about social change as an occupation took root, at least within certain idealistic circles. When I recently heard the phrase "professional organizer," it was a slur, not a compliment.

Notably, too, this was the era of the right-wing backlash, the toxic blast of union bashing, deregulation, and financialization that led to the explosion of income inequality that the left has been incapable of mitigating—incapable in part because of the turn away from economic justice to other causes, but also because the left has been up against an extraordinary adversary. Conservatives were busy executing organizational strategies during the last third of the twentieth century—launching think tanks and business associations buoyed by corporate largesse, inflaming the ground troops of the Moral Majority, and laying the foundation for a permanent tax revolt by the 1 percent—even as the left was abandoning its organizing roots.

Yet organizing is what the left must cultivate to make its activism more durable and effective, to sustain and advance our causes when the galvanizing intensity of occupations or street protests subsides. It is what the left needs in order to roll back the conservative resurgence and cut down plutocracy. That means founding political organizations, hashing out long-term strategies, cultivating leaders (of the accountable, not charismatic, variety), and figuring out how to support them financially. No doubt the thriving of activism in recent decades is a good thing, and activism is something we want more of. The problem, rather, is that the organizing that made earlier movements successful has failed to grow apace.

* * *

In the sixties, Rudd, Dunbar-Ortiz, and their respective cohorts learned about organizing almost by osmosis, absorbing a model "developed and tested over many generations," as Rudd put it. (Their ambient awareness of organizing, Rudd clarified in his talk, informed the years of preparation that made the celebrated 1968 Columbia occupation possible; ignoring those efforts in a fit of hubris is where the Weather Underground went wrong.) Today's activists have come of age in a very different milieu. No one has a parent in the

Communist Party, trade unions are in terminal decline, and the protracted struggle of the civil rights movement, which has so much to teach us, has been reduced to a series of iconic images and feel-good history highlights.

To be an activist now merely means to advocate for change, and the *how*s and *why*s of that advocacy are unclear. The lack of a precise antonym is telling. Who, exactly, are the nonactivists? Are they passivists? Spectators? Or just regular people? In its very ambiguity the word upholds a dichotomy that is toxic to democracy, which depends on the participation of an active citizenry, not the zealotry of a small segment of the population, to truly function.

As my friend Jonathan Matthew Smucker, whom I met at Zuccotti Park during the early days of Occupy Wall Street, argues, the term *activist* is suspiciously devoid of content. "Labels are certainly not new to collective political action," Smucker writes in *Hegemony How-To*, pointing to classifications like *abolitionist, populist, suffragette, unionist,* and *socialist,* which all convey a clear position on an issue. But *activist* is a generic category associated with oddly specific stereotypes: today, the term signals not so much a certain set of political opinions or behaviors as a certain temperament. In our increasingly sorted and labeled society, activists are analogous to skateboarders or foodies or Deadheads, each inhabiting a particular niche in this nation's grand and heterogeneous cultural ecosystem—by some quirk of personality, they enjoy long meetings, shouting slogans, and spending a night or two in jail the way others may savor a glass of biodynamic wine. Worse still, Smucker contends, is the fact that many activists seem to relish their marginalization, interpreting their small numbers as evidence of their specialness, their membership in an exclusive and righteous clique, effectiveness be damned.

While there are notable exceptions, many strands of contemporary activism risk emphasizing the self over the collective. By contrast, organizing is cooperative by definition: it aims to bring others into the fold, to build and exercise shared power. Organizing, as Smucker smartly defines it, involves turning "a social bloc into a political force." Today, anyone can be an activist, even someone who operates alone, accountable to no one—for example, relentlessly trying to raise awareness about an important issue. Raising awareness—one of contemporary activism's preferred aims—can be extremely valuable (at least I hope so, since I have spent so much time trying to do it). But education is not organizing, which involves not just enlightening whoever happens to encounter your message, but also aggregating people around common interests so that they can strategically wield their combined strength. Organizing is long-term and often tedious work that entails creating infrastructure and institutions, finding points of vulnerability and leverage in the situation you want to transform, and convincing atomized individuals to recognize that they are on the same team and to behave like it.

Globally, we've seen an explosion of social movements since 2011, yet many of us involved in them remain trapped in the basic bind Rudd described. "Activism, the expression of our deeply held feelings, used to be only one part of building a movement. It's a tactic which has been elevated to the level of strategy, in the absence of strategy," he lamented. "Most young activists think organizing means making the physical arrangements for a rally or benefit concert." Add to this list creating a social media hashtag, circulating an online petition, and debating people on the internet, and the sentiment basically holds. The work of organizing has fallen out of esteem within many movement circles, where a faith in spontaneous rebellion and a deep suspicion of institutions, leadership, and taking power are entrenched.

That isn't to say that there aren't times when rallies, concerts, hashtags, petitions, and online debates are useful—they sometimes are. The problem is that these events or tactics too often represent the horizon of political engagement. "I think it's generally a good thing that large numbers of people have been inspired in recent decades to take action, and that developments in technology have made it easier for them to do so," said L. A. Kauffman, author of *Direct Action: Protest and the Reinvention of American Radicalism*. "Divorced from a deliberate organizing strategy, all of this can just be a flurry of activity without much impact, of course, so we return to the need for our movements to recognize and cultivate organizing talent, and to support this work by treating it as work—e.g., by finding ways to pay people a living wage to do it." To state what should be self-evident, when people take small concrete actions—signing a petition or showing up at a rally, for example—the actions are more likely to have a real influence when guided by a clear game plan, ideally one with the objective of inconveniencing elites and impeding their profits.

* * *

Obviously, there are still organizers in the classic mold—labor organizers, in particular—doing invaluable work. And a growing number of people are experimenting with new forms of collective economic power and resistance. But one major challenge in these neoliberal and post-Fordist times is to find inventive ways to update the union model for our current conditions of financialization and insecurity. We need to create fresh ties among the millions of stranded people who lack stable employment, let alone union membership, so that they become a force to be reckoned with. I have been part of an effort, born of the chaos of Occupy Wall Street, which attempts to do this by organizing people around indebtedness. The project, which launched the nation's first student debt strike in 2015, recognizes that debt is money, a tradable asset for the financial class, and a source of leverage for those stuck in the red. We take inspiration from the old adage "If you owe the bank $100, that's your problem. If you owe the bank $100 million, that's the bank's problem."

Other efforts are much further along. Climate justice organizers have devised original ways to mobilize people to affect oil companies' bottom lines—by forcing the federal government to stop issuing new coal mining leases on public land, for example. Since launching in 2012, the campaign for fossil fuel divestment has managed to pressure investors controlling more than $14 trillion in assets to exit the market. Organizing started with students on campuses and then expanded to include citizens of broader communities, with a growing list of cities and towns worldwide now pledged to support full or partial divestment. "One of the greatest successes of the divestment campaign thus far has been to undermine confidence in the fossil fuel industry's business plan," Jamie Henn, a cofounder of the environmental group 350.org and one of the campaign leaders, told me. "Now it's not just small liberal arts colleges that are taking 'carbon risk' seriously, but huge financial institutions like the Bank of England, the Norwegian Sovereign Wealth Fund, and California's pension systems."

Finally, there is the Black Lives Matter movement, which has done an astounding job of putting racial oppression back on the national agenda. Groups like the Dream Defenders, a Florida outfit that coalesced in the wake of Trayvon Martin's murder, have embraced a model of "leaderful" as opposed to "leaderless" organizing, while taking a skeptical approach to online-only activism. "To change our communities, we must have power, not just followers," the group's leaders explained after a ten-week, strategy-focused social media hiatus. While concrete victories have been few and far between, the Movement for Black Lives achieved a remarkable win in 2015 when the University of Missouri football team threatened to go on strike for the rest of the season unless the school president, Tim Wolfe, stepped down. And he did.

This phenomenal show of economic might—the cancellation of one game would have cost the university $1 million dollars—was quickly blotted out, however, by a raging debate over free speech on campus, driven by an unfortunate encounter between a Missouri professor and a young journalist and by subsequent events at Yale, where students took understandable umbrage at a faculty member's preemptive defense of racist Halloween costumes. As the debate over free speech raged in op-ed sections and Facebook threads, some rightly observed that the shift of focus was distracting. Pundits started talking about the First Amendment and stopped talking about systemic racism. They also stopped talking about the reasons the Missouri athletes' form of direct action got the goods and how their approach to organizing might be replicated elsewhere.

* * *

All things considered, the word *activist* isn't that bad. It is, at the very least, certainly preferable to *social entrepreneur*, *change agent*, or—god forbid—*social justice warrior*. Unlike *activist*, with its hazy etymology, the history of *social justice warrior*, or SJW, can be traced in remarkable detail thanks to the website Know Your Meme. It first appeared in a blog post on November 6, 2009, and by April 21, 2011, merited its own entry on Urban Dictionary: "A pejorative term for an individual who repeatedly and vehemently engages in arguments on social justice on the Internet, often in a shallow or not well-thought-out way, for the purpose of raising their own personal reputation."

Since then, the expression has traveled up the media food chain, from Reddit and 4chan to the *Daily Beast*, *Slate*, the *New York Times*, and *Salon*, which argued that "progressives should embrace the term." The rapid mainstreaming found momentum in a wave of campus unrest. The *New York Post* editorial board, for example, warned that "Social Justice Warriors now rule at the University of Missouri." While the piece mentions the football players, the real focus was, predictably, the alleged suppression of free speech. "The quest for 'safe spaces' is starting to look a lot like fascism," the editors opined. In 2020 they were still beating the same drum. "Social Justice Warriors Are Waging a Dangerous 'Cancel Cultural Revolution,'" one headline blared.

So there we have it. A century ago, the idea of activism was born of a philosopher—Eucken—who preferred the mystical to the material, and that preference still lingers on today, for many still believe that action, even when disconnected from any coherent strategy, can magically lead to a kind of societal awakening. Social justice warfare, in turn, emerged from some of the internet's more unsavory recesses as an insult concocted to belittle those who take issue with bigotry. But vitriol aside, the term betrays a faith that unites social justice warriors and their critics (a faith, to be clear, that is all too common today): that voicing opinions and arguing with strangers online is a form of political engagement as significant as planning a picket, boycott, or strike.

Fortunately, at least for now, social justice warriors have not totally eclipsed activists, and activists have not completely eradicated organizers. There are still plenty of arenas in which real organizing—what Rudd described in his talk as "education, base-building, and coalition," and what I would describe as creating collective identity and shared economic power—is being done, but these slow-moving efforts are often overshadowed by the latest spectacle or viral outrage.

In 2016, a decade after I sat listening to Mark Rudd speak in a dingy room, tens of thousands of people flocked to auditoriums far and wide to hear presidential hopeful Bernie Sanders condemn the "billionaire class." At that time, polls began to show that a growing number of young people and the majority of Democratic primary voters had a positive view of socialism. Since then, we have seen an encouraging revival of dedicated organizing that aims to channel this astonishing uptick in leftist sentiment into lasting power in the electoral realm and beyond, from the impressive work of the youth-led Sunrise Movement fighting for a Green New Deal to the expanding membership of the Democratic Socialists of America to the surge in worker-led resistance and labor union activity in fields ranging from teaching to Big Tech.

Day by day, the word *organizer* is becoming more esteemed. Semantics alone will not determine history's course, for it matters less what we call ourselves and more what we do, but often the language we use doesn't help the cause. It has always been easy for elites to dismiss as losers and malcontents those who challenge them, but it takes even less effort to ignore a meme. Successful organizers, by contrast, are more difficult to shrug off because they have built a base that acts strategically. The goal of any would-be world-changer should be to be part of something so organized, so formidable, and so shrewd that the powerful don't scoff, they quake.

4

WIPE THE SLATE CLEAN

On September 2, 2020, the anthropologist and activist David Graeber died unexpectedly, while on holiday in Venice. David, who was my friend and collaborator for more than a decade, was best known for his groundbreaking study *Debt: The First 5,000 Years*, published in 2011. The book opened up a vibrant and ongoing conversation about the evolution of our economic system by challenging conventional accounts of the origins of money and markets. Relationships of credit and debt, he showed, preceded the development of coinage and cash. The book also influenced a movement for debt cancellation, which appears poised on the brink of a significant victory that could improve untold millions of lives. I only wish my friend could be around to see it.

Debt's publication was perfectly timed to lend scholarly legitimacy to the frustration that fueled Occupy Wall Street, an uprising David helped catalyze. He recruited me to the effort, and then invited me to join an offshoot focused on debt resistance. One meeting led to another, and then another. We

---

* Previously published as "How the Biden Administration Can Free Americans from Student Debt," *New Yorker*, November 23, 2020.

worked together on a range of experiments, including a radical financial-literacy guide called *The Debt Resistors' Operations Manual* and the Rolling Jubilee. That set the stage for the Debt Collective, the union for debtors I helped found.

Since 2014, the Debt Collective has been working to let the world know that any US president, should they desire, can make every penny of federal student debt disappear without consulting Congress (and regardless of Mitch McConnell's objections). Based on legal research, Debt Collective cofounder Luke Herrine and Harvard Law School's Eileen Connor argue that Congress granted legal authority to the head of the Department of Education to extinguish federal student-loan debt, an action called "compromise and settlement," in 1965. All a president has to do is instruct the education secretary to use this authority to cancel all federal student debt. Our public-education campaign caught on. In September 2020, senators Elizabeth Warren and Chuck Schumer offered a Senate resolution urging the incoming president to cancel up to $50,000 in student loans for every borrower, using compromise-and-settlement authority. Explaining her rationale, Warren told me over email that getting rid of student debt "would give a big, consumer-driven boost to our economy and even help close the Black-white wealth gap."

As the 2020 presidential race wore on, Joe Biden shifted his position on the issue of debt forgiveness, proposing to "forgive all undergraduate tuition-related federal student debt from two- and four-year public colleges and universities for debt-holders earning up to $125,000." Biden also promised to "immediately cancel a minimum of $10,000 of student debt per person," as part of a coronavirus response. Within hours of the major networks declaring Biden triumphant over Donald Trump, social media resounded with discussion of the president-elect's ability to eliminate student loans using executive authority. "Joe Biden embraced progressive demands for student debt cancellation after he won the Democratic nomination," Bloomberg reported. "Whether he agrees to use executive authority to grant loan relief will test how much influence progressives hold in his administration."

Amid a daunting public-health and economic crisis, a loudening chorus of experts and elected officials believe that a more ambitious approach to debt relief is needed to stem the suffering. The Debt Collective has long promoted a sweeping jubilee, a mass cancellation of debts, including but not limited to the abolition of all federal student debt. Without offering precise sums, a white paper from the Roosevelt Institute, a progressive think tank, advocates for the cancellation of student, housing, and medical debt as part of a broader Covid-recovery plan. In Congress, the representatives known as the Squad have lifted up grassroots demands to cancel student loans, back rent, and mortgage payments. Debt relief, Representative Ayanna Pressley of Massachusetts told me, makes sound economic sense, given that working families would put freed-up money "right back into communities, right back into the economy." Pressley added, "We have to bail out the American people."

Though it would help struggling households make ends meet, debt relief isn't just about money. There are also deeper moral questions to consider—and this is where David Graeber's work is indispensable. In *Debt*, he sought to challenge his readers to rethink the very notion of owing. Who owes what to whom? Do all debts need to be repaid? Can our real obligations ever be quantified? As an anthropologist who had studied gift exchange, and an anarchist determined to envision a world beyond capitalism, David wanted to help build a world unconstrained by the constant and petty accounting of debits and credits, one where value and worth were not denominated in dollars. Debt, he wrote, is "a promise corrupted by both math and violence." What other types of promises might we make to one another and strive to honor? And, in order to do that, what promises might we have to renegotiate or refuse?

* * *

Before the pandemic, US indebtedness was breaking records: in 2019, total household debt in the United States surpassed $14 trillion; total student-loan debt alone surpassed $1.6 trillion. More than a million people defaulted on their federal educational loans every year between 2015 and 2019. Experts have bemoaned the consequences of mass insolvency, which suppresses demand for other goods and services, impeding homeownership and increasing household insecurity. There are physical and psychological consequences, too. Being behind on bills stresses body and mind, a tendency exacerbated by the fact that debtors tend to delay or avoid seeking medical care, fearful of the cost. Data from the credit bureau Experian in December 2016 showed that the average American died $62,000 in arrears.

At the close of 2020, with Trump's freeze on student-loan payments and the Centers for Disease Control and Prevention's halt on evictions about to expire, a debt-addled humanitarian disaster loomed. Countless families teetering on the edge of financial collapse were about to be pushed over the brink. People spent 30 percent of their stimulus checks to service debts, and as back rent piled up, some forty million households were at risk of homelessness. "Without immediate and effective stabilization, we could see long-term debt and bankruptcy spirals—starting with middle- and low-income Americans," the Nobel Prize–winning economist Joseph Stiglitz warned. Of course, not all debtors are equally desperate; some are treated better than others. The persistence of the racial wealth gap and predatory lending practices means that Black and Latinx communities tend to be more economically precarious and indebted than their white counterparts. Black women are the most burdened by student-loan debt, and often have to resort to payday loans with onerous terms. The ensuing economic fallout of Covid-19 meant the same communities disproportionately ravaged by the disease were also dealt an economic death blow, compounding the damage wrought by the mortgage crisis. According to a Pew Research Center analysis, between 2005 and 2009, the median wealth among Black and Latinx households fell by more than 50 percent.

Debt cancellation is an essential component of any sensible response to such a disaster, especially one attuned to questions of racial justice. A sense of justice, however, rarely guides our financial agreements. As David observed in *Debt*, money has the capacity "to turn morality into a matter of impersonal arithmetic—and by doing so, to justify things that would otherwise seem outrageous or obscene." Think of the Florida law passed by the state's Republican-controlled legislature in 2019, and later upheld by a federal appeals court, which requires former felons to fully pay back their court fines and fees in order to vote; the federal government's habit of garnishing Social Security payments if recipients have defaulted on their federal student loans; or the fact that some small children are denied meals by public schools because their families owe lunch debt. We rarely question the moral logic that enables such obscenities—logic that views the debtors as culpable, even criminal, and thus deserving of punishment. The German word *Schuld*, David was fond of pointing out, means both debt and guilt.

Debt is a power relationship built on the pretense of equality. In theory, a debtor and creditor enter into a contract on a level playing field and with fair terms; in reality, debts are often incurred under conditions of duress. Right now, countless people are putting expenses on credit cards or taking out high-interest payday loans because they've lost their jobs or unemployment benefits have dried up (or never came through). As the Debt Collective writes in its manifesto, *Can't Pay, Won't Pay: The Case for Economic Disobedience and Debt Abolition*, "Most people are not in debt because they live beyond their means; they are in debt because they have been denied the means to live." In countries with universal health care, individual medical debt is rare; in the United States, it is a leading cause of poverty and the main catalyst for bankruptcy. In some cases, failure to appear in court for unpaid medical debts lands people in jail. No one chooses to get sick, so why is medical debt something people should feel bad about, let alone be penalized or incarcerated for? This is why, following David's lead, the Debt Collective rejects the language of debt "forgiveness"—which implies a blameworthy borrower and a beneficent creditor—in favor of challenging the underlying morality of a system in which millions must take on debt in order to survive.

In modern economic life, you can count on moral judgment being inconsistently applied. There is, as Pressley told me, "a glaring double standard when it comes to consumer versus corporate debtors." It is a double standard perfectly captured in a popular meme that invites people to list things that are considered "classy" if an individual is rich and "trashy" if that person is poor. Bankruptcy is frequently mentioned, along with being bilingual and having someone else raise your kids. The more privileged you are, the more debt can work to your advantage, and the same can hold true for defaulting. That's certainly the case for Donald Trump, who left a trail of corporate bankruptcies in his wake and ended his presidency on the hook for hundreds of millions of dollars.

High levels of corporate debt are, we mustn't forget, one reason we are in this mess. For more than a decade, companies took advantage of low interest rates and gorged themselves on credit, often using the funds to buy back stock and push out dividends to shareholders, rather than raising employee wages or saving for a rainy day. These overleveraged companies made our economy more vulnerable to the coronavirus shock. And yet their behavior is rewarded. In spring 2020, the Federal Reserve decided to purchase corporate debt, including the junk bonds, or riskier debt, issued by companies whose investment ratings had plummeted because of the pandemic—the so-called fallen angels. Regular debtors, in contrast, are rarely shown such charity; instead of being heralded as divine, they are dubbed deadbeats.

By offering more support to corporate borrowers and lenders, the Fed bolstered the bond market in an unprecedented way, and encouraged more of the bad behavior that paved the way for the crisis, potentially setting the stage for a bigger catastrophe down the road. The world's largest companies rushed to take advantage of the new arrangement, with entities including Alphabet and Apple (which, in August 2020, became the first company to be valued at more than $2 trillion) borrowing billions at preposterously low rates. "Junk" debt also got a boost, with some companies that are seen as risky investments now able to pay out less than 3 percent on their bonds, Alexis Goldstein, a senior policy analyst at Americans for Financial Reform, told me. For corporations, we saw a remarkable lowering of the price to borrow money, but we did not see anything equivalent for people at the margins of our financial markets—or some municipalities in desperate need of funds. "We've seen lots of people being able to refinance their homes, but those are people who tend to be in a good financial position," Goldstein explained. They own their homes instead of renting and have the stable incomes required to qualify for low rates. "People that need a payday loan are not seeing lower rates of payday loans. People who are having to use their credit cards to avoid eviction, the people who are at the most risk of financial ruin right now, are not seeing the lowering of interest rates." If you look at your credit card information, you'll find that your interest rate is likely far higher than 3 percent.

The Fed soothed skittish markets, but at what cost? There was very little conditionality attached to its acquisition of corporate debt, which means that, even though Wall Street was buoyed, no guaranteed benefits trickled down to workers in need. The CARES Act granted the Fed discretionary authority to "require corporations receiving rescue aid to retain jobs, maintain collective bargaining agreements, prohibit dividends and stock buybacks, and limit executive compensation," wrote Amanda Fischer of the Washington Center for Equitable Growth. But the Fed did not impose such conditions on corporate borrowers. Instead, the Fed bought the corporate debt of companies such as Tyson Foods, a meat-processing company that has become infamous for its Covid-19 outbreaks, and ExxonMobil, which chose to lay off workers instead of reducing payouts to shareholders. These actions create the true moral hazard where debt is concerned, insulating businesses from the downsides of their recklessness by ensuring the public picks up the tab.

* * *

The question of whether debts always have to be repaid has preoccupied political thinkers going back millennia. Plato's *Republic*, written in the fourth century BCE, ponders this question. According to Socrates, "paying your debts is not a correct definition of justice." Much later, Thomas Jefferson fulminated against debt as an unjust encumbrance on posterity, arguing for the abolition of debts unpaid after this "natural limit," which he took to be the span of a generation. But he did not call for mercy across the board. In an 1803 letter, Jefferson recommended wielding debt as a tool to dispossess Indigenous people of their territory: "We shall push our trading houses, and be glad to see the good and influential individuals among them run in debt, because we observe that when these debts get beyond what the individuals can pay, they become willing to lop them off by a cessation of lands."

The question of whether debts must be repaid is always also a question of who will pay them. Will creditors and landlords at the top of the income scale be able to collect in full, or will debtors and renters at the bottom earn a reprieve? In *Debt*, David recounts that, in the ancient world, bad harvests and warfare repeatedly pushed farmers into debt peonage, or even debt slavery, threatening social stability. To prevent total

calamity, Sumerian and Babylonian kings announced peri-
odic amnesties. "These were called 'declarations of freedom,'"
David wrote, noting that the "Sumerian word *amargi*, the
first recorded word for 'freedom' in any known human language, literally means 'return to mother'—since this is what
freed debt-peons were finally allowed to do." The economist
Michael Hudson points to the Code of Hammurabi, dating
to 1750 BCE, which aimed to restore economic normalcy after major disruptions: the forty-eighth law proclaims "a debt
and tax amnesty for cultivators if Adad the Storm God had
flooded their fields, or if their crops failed as a result of pests
or drought."

As the historical record shows, debt relief is not a utopian
demand. In the modern era, more than a million loans were
granted by the Home Owners' Loan Corporation to rescue
homeowners with distressed mortgages during the Great
Depression. Today, a full student-debt jubilee would be an
obvious place to start. Eileen Connor, of Harvard Law School,
was unequivocal about President Joe Biden's ability to eliminate all student debt by executive action: "The legal authority
is there. And the moral justification is there, too." She pointed
to the "growing recognition that student-loan debt entrenches
structural inequalities, especially racial inequality." Research
shows that a full student-debt jubilee would help close the
racial wealth gap, because the burden of student debt falls disproportionately on borrowers of color. (A 2019 study reported
that, twenty years after starting college, the median white student owes 6 percent of their cumulative federal student loans,
or around $1,000, while the median Black student still owes
95 percent, or around $18,500.) There are also urgent eco-
nomic incentives for widespread debt relief. Full student-debt

cancellation, a 2018 analysis estimated, could potentially boost the economy by as much as $108 billion a year, with the benefits reaching far beyond the nearly forty-five million people directly burdened by student loans.

A growing number of economists argue that we can't afford *not* to cancel debt. As the title of a *Washington Post* op-ed by Hudson in March 2020 bluntly put it, "A Debt Jubilee Is the Only Way to Avoid a Depression." Richard Vague, the secretary of banking and securities for the state of Pennsylvania, laid out concrete proposals to restructure mortgage debt, student loans, health-care debt, and small-business loans. "Whether called 'restructuring,' 'forgiveness,' or 'jubilee,'" Vague wrote, "it is the only feasible way to reduce private sector debt when it accumulates to crushing levels in societies, and the only way to do so without severely damaging the economy."

Biden—a former senator from Delaware (the credit card capital of the world) and a driving force behind a controversial 2005 bill that stripped student borrowers of bankruptcy protections—will need to be pushed to stand up for debtors. Grassroots pressure is building to that end. In June 2020, the Movement for Black Lives called for the absolution of student loans, medical debt, mortgage payments, and rent. Tenant unions across the country rallied to cancel rent. In July 2020, the Poor People's Campaign, cochaired by the Reverend Dr. William Barber and the Reverend Dr. Liz Theoharis, issued a "Jubilee Platform" that includes various forms of debt cancellation. On the first day of the Biden-Harris administration, the Debt Collective launched a student loan strike, the Biden Jubilee 100, building on the success of our previous strike campaign and demanding that the president immediately abolish all federal student loan debt using compromise-and-settlement authority. Why should ordinary people honor their debts when the rich walk away from theirs without remorse? If corporations are people, why would they be more entitled to debt cancellation?

Instead of sinking and struggling alone and ashamed, debtors are beginning to take a page out of the creditors' playbook and lobby for their shared interests in order to challenge the phony morality that upholds an untenable status quo.

* * *

The month before David Graeber died, I reread *Debt*, in anticipation of a dialogue that we had planned to record and publish in September 2020. This time, I found the uncompromising, radical vision at its center even more striking. *Debt* does more than challenge the reader to rethink the old shibboleth that all debts must be repaid—it questions the very notion of debt itself.

"On one level the difference between an obligation and a debt is simple and obvious," David writes. "A debt is the obligation to pay a certain sum of money. As a result, a debt, unlike any other form of obligation, can be precisely quantified. This allows debts to become simple, cold, and impersonal—which, in turn, allows them to be transferable." Although obligations to family and friends are nontransferable, a loan at a set interest rate is an asset that can be securitized and traded. By adhering to the logic of compound interest, debt crowds out more indefinite obligations, commitments that can't be paid back in cash and can only be met with respect, gratitude, generosity, and care. Many of us feel indebted to our parents, for example, but that doesn't mean we can write them a check as payback for bringing us into the world.

We are all, David reminds us, caught up in relationships in which the balance sheet is never wholly settled—simultaneously debtors and creditors, in countless small exchanges. Our everyday language reveals this: the English "much obliged" and the Portuguese *obrigado* mean "I am in your debt," while the French *de rien* and Spanish *de nada* assure others that it is nothing. To say "my pleasure" is to claim that an action is, in fact, a credit—you did me a favor by giving me an opportunity to be kind.

Credit, of course, is the flip side of debt. Etymologically, the term conjures trust, and extending trust to others is the basis of sociability. "The story of the origins of capitalism," David writes, "is not the story of the gradual destruction of traditional communities by the impersonal power of the market. It is, rather, the story of how an economy of credit was converted into an economy of interest." What if, instead of believing the myth that we are guilty debtors, we saw ourselves also as creditors—as human beings entitled to a dignified, secure, and flourishing life? What if our societies really do owe us all an equal living?

In David's view, the slate must periodically be wiped clean so that we can free ourselves from debt as both an economic burden and as an ideology that shapes and distorts our interactions. For now, debt pervades our thinking, even when we aspire to change things. As protests for racial justice are likely to continue in response to police brutality, it is often said that we are living through a moment of reckoning. This word is telling: to reckon means "to calculate," or "to establish by counting or calculation"—as in, my dictionary tells me, "His debts were reckoned at $300,000." Given the scale of the harm, it is impossible to truly reckon with the legacy of slavery and structural racism in this way, which is why leaders of the movement for reparations for the Atlantic slave trade often oppose attempts to assign a number to the debt, arguing instead that it is so vast it necessitates a reordering of international relations. Or consider the announcement by the city of Louisville, Kentucky, that it would pay more than $12 million to the family of Breonna Taylor, a young woman killed by the police during a botched raid on her apartment, as though any sum could encapsulate her life's worth. Certainly, monetary compensation is important, but the state also has an obligation to ensure that what happened to Taylor never happens again. "If people are really serious about a national reckoning on racial injustice," Ayanna Pressley told me, "the only receipts that matter to mitigate the existing hurt and to chart a new path forward are our budgets and our policies."

David Graeber believed that we might one day free ourselves from the tyranny of debt to embrace a more expansive economic paradigm. As an anthropologist, he understood the enormous variation and inherent mutability of human society and cultural traditions. Financial contracts can be rewritten, and social contracts can be remade, as well. That's what grassroots movements do, pushing against vested interests that, when under enough pressure, typically prefer half measures to profound transformation. In *Debt*, David remarked that, even when plagued by debt crises, ancient Athens and Rome "insisted on legislating around the edges." The United States has done something similar, he wrote, eliminating some of the most egregious abuses, including debtors' prisons, but never having challenged "the principle of debt itself."

Even though I have spent years organizing for a mass jubilee, I too have held on to the idea that some debts are legitimate, and that what we need is a sort of moral audit to separate the odious from the upright. I wanted to ask David about this during the conversation we had planned. Now that he's gone, I feel like I'm beginning to grasp his deeper point. How could I ever pay back what I owe him? My debt goes beyond what numbers or words can convey. The only way I can honor my obligation is to continue fighting for the transformed world he wanted to see.

5

RECLAIMING THE FUTURE

In early 2019, I found myself seated onstage, rather incongruously, between the neoconservative Never-Trumper
turned "Resistance" hero Bill Kristol and my friend Natasha
Lennard, a radical antifascist writer and activist I first met at
Occupy Wall Street back in 2011. We had all made our way
to the New School for the closing panel of "Liberalism and
Democracy: Past, Present, Prospects," a conference organized
by professors James Miller and Helena Rosenblatt, authors
of *Can Democracy Work?* and *The Lost History of Liberalism*,
respectively, which they had recently published. The audience
was mainly academics and graduate students, with a few jour-
nalists thrown in for good measure; the atmosphere decidedly
more rarefied than rabble-rousing.

The two-day confab had opened with a screening of my
film *What Is Democracy?*, a philosophical documentary that
put one of the conference's main themes—democracy understood as collective self-rule—front and center. But where the
film makes the case for democracy's deepening and expansion

---

* Previously published as "Reclaiming the Future: On the Growing
Appeal of Socialism in an Age of Inequality," *New Republic*, May 17, 2019.

beyond electoral politics into areas such as workplaces, schools, the health sector, the economy, and the home, the majority of the event's presenters went on to emphasize the mandate to contain democracy's growth within the bounds circumscribed by the conference's other organizing idea, liberalism.

After the credits rolled, the esteemed historian Ira Katznelson took the podium. Elegantly breaking down the distinction between the two intertwined terms, he paraphrased Alexis de Tocqueville: "A democratic people rule as God reigns in the universe." Liberalism, Katznelson continued, is an altogether different beast from democracy—one more attuned to, and wary of, human beings' less-than-divine tendencies. As a set of political guardrails, liberalism aims to protect individuals from predatory rulers while also preventing the multitude from becoming a mob. "Democracy advances, and liberalism restrains, popular sovereignty by creating means, familiar to Americans, that include staggered and mediated elections, a free press, religious liberty, judicial review, federalism, the separation of powers," he explained.

"If we want to live inside a decent political order," Katznelson confidently declared, "there is no better option on offer" than liberal democracy. But his lecture had concluded on a downbeat note, for liberal democracy now finds its star fading, dimmed by challengers from various corners: from ethno-nationalist pseudo-populism and illiberal autocrats in countries such as Hungary and Brazil to authoritarian capitalism offering economic growth without political freedom in China. It's also been challenged by resurgent socialism in places like the United Kingdom and even, astonishingly enough, the United States.

* * *

After decades of exile from mainstream political discourse, the word *socialism* is now emblazoned in headlines and getting serious (if not always respectful) hearings from politicians holding and seeking the highest offices of the land. Even people who were not fans of Vermont senator and presidential hopeful Bernie Sanders (though a surprising number were and are fans—he is consistently in the running for the most popular politician in the country) cheered the arrival of two democratic socialist powerhouses in Congress, Alexandria Ocasio-Cortez of the Bronx and Detroit representative Rashida Tlaib. Their victories were higher profile, but no less significant, than those at the state and municipal level—from Houston, where a democratic socialist judge won his campaign, to Chicago, where six of fifty city council seats were won by socialists. Philadelphia Democratic ward leader Nikil Saval decided to embark on his successful campaign for state senate when he realized political space had opened for him to campaign as who he really is—a socialist. It's a development he could have scarcely foreseen a few years prior.

This leftward momentum also nudged long-standing bastions of liberalism, be they magazines like the *New Republic* or the younger wing of the Democratic Party, to take socialism seriously, while also compelling the federal government to respond. "Detailed policy proposals from self-declared socialists are gaining support in Congress and among much of the younger electorate," warned the Council of Economic Advisers in its 2018 white paper, "The Opportunity Costs of Socialism"—a stern alarm that's echoed across countless think pieces and pundit panels. The convergence of stubbornly stagnant incomes, unpayable student loans, unaffordable housing and health care, racist policing systems, entrenched misogyny, and a looming climate catastrophe has displaced long-standing political certainties in the United States. Now a growing wave of millennial radicalism—together, of course, with a nativist lurch toward authoritarianism on the right—has put the liberal tradition on the defensive.

The old liberal consensus issued from the blithe insistence that the marriage between democracy and capitalism, between free elections and freeish markets, was a charmed and stable union that would yield prosperity and justice everywhere. Those foundational precepts look more and more fanciful as acute conditions of economic inequality and democratic deficit continue to deepen. Many establishment liberals still hope that the partnership between untrammeled capitalism and liberal democracy can be patched up, but a growing and restive chorus of radical and reformist voices roots for their separation. People are beginning to say long-unspeakable thoughts aloud: If we want to salvage democracy and many of the liberal rights and protections we associate with it, we'll have to do more than reform or temper capitalism. We must find a way, rather, to jettison and transcend it.

In *The Communist Manifesto*, Karl Marx and Friedrich Engels famously wrote about "the specter of communism" haunting Europe. And at the "Liberalism and Democracy" conference, it seemed fitting that socialism appeared mostly as a spectral presence—like a path long ago taken to be a dead end now appearing eerily on the horizon. The assembled scholars seemed to believe that the American public needed to be reminded that history had ended some three decades past—that the ideological contents of lapsed Cold War battles had been long consigned to history's dustbin, and the road to socialism blocked off. They turned to the challenge with manifest enthusiasm.

The title of the conference's closing panel drove this terminal message home. "The Last Best Hope of Earth" (emphasis on *last*) clearly referred to liberal democracy, as Marc Plattner, coeditor of the *Journal of Democracy*, made explicit in his opening commentary. Whatever liberal democracy's shortcomings might be, he argued, "the alternatives are always worse, and often unspeakably worse." Citizens, he warned, are "likely to undervalue the imperfect freedom and equality delivered by their imperfect liberal democracies." As a result, "the blessings of liberal democracies are too often discounted, especially by those who have never experienced life under other kinds of regimes." Bill Kristol weighed in next, questioning the wisdom of ordinary citizens, who, in his estimation, tend to undervalue the liberty he and other conservatives understand as the core tenet of liberalism. (An early and credulous champion of the disastrous occupation of Iraq and the conservative tactician who'd been more responsible than anyone else for Sarah Palin's elevation to the national stage, Kristol did not acknowledge that elites conspired to deceive the public into supporting the war; nor did he mention that voters were not foolish enough to heed his advice and send Palin to the White House.)

Taken together, their remarks were emblematic of liberalism's apprehensive response to mounting pressure from the left. In my own comments from the podium, I tried to dispel two stubborn misconceptions about today's socialist revival. First, its adherents do not criticize liberal democracy because they discount its vaunted rights and freedoms, but because they seek to create the conditions under which such principles might at last be fully enacted and ideally expanded. (You're far more likely to hear young socialists talk about enhancing democratic processes by, say, enfranchising felons or making Election Day a national holiday than promoting a vanguard-led dictatorship of the proletariat.) Second, the central political and social challenges we now face stem not from the fabled "tyranny of the majority"—the wayward passions of the masses—but from the impunity of a greedy and blinkered minority. This model of oligarchic rule is epitomized by the world's handful of billionaires who possess as much wealth as fully half of the world's population—or by the five people on the Supreme Court determined to use their judicial authority to impose a conservative agenda on a resistant population. Poll after poll shows that the bulk of citizens, often in overwhelming numbers, are pro-immigrant, would prefer a public option for health care, want background checks for gun purchases, favor much higher taxes on the wealthy, support swift and serious action on climate change, and want to end wars, but these positions do not reflect what our leaders deliver.

It's fashionable in pundit circles to frame our current political moment as "populist"—an explanatory frame that allows for a false equivalency between the left and the right, and paints the excessive and unruly passions of common citizens as the predominant threat to political stability. In reality, however, our core social problems stem not from a misguided people but from unaccountable plutocrats who have rigged the rules of the game in order to veto substantive popular reform. "Democracy advances, liberalism restrains," Katznelson said. But the socialist wing of our politics and its growing retinue of fellow travelers are asking just who is being restrained: the people or the powerful? What good is liberalism if it enables power to follow property at the expense of a forward-looking popular will?

Even the most basic liberal democratic right—the right to vote, about which there is no end to sanctimony in this country—has never been equitably put into practice. Gaze upon our system's vaunted political blessings from the perspective of, say, someone in Puerto Rico, and they look even more mixed than they do from the mainland, where the Constitution places more weight on rural votes and less-populated regions by design. Hurricane Maria in 2017 left more than three thousand dead, not because of the force of the storm but because of inadequate, underfunded infrastructure that still has not been repaired. This state of malign neglect exists in part because island residents, US citizens though they may be, lack representation in Congress and have no electoral votes to influence the presidency. Our country's other supposedly sacred right, free speech, means little when the Supreme Court has repeatedly decided that spending money merits First Amendment protections. Rather than reflecting a desire to ditch liberal rights, the turn toward democratic socialism is born of the recognition that liberal principles are not strong enough to survive, let alone constrain, concentrated economic power. And absent any such robust constraints, the forces that the first capital-*P* Populists of the 1890s dubbed the Money Power will inevitably seek to undermine the basic freedoms regular people fought and died to win.

Looking back on the New School event, I'm tempted to riff on Plattner's statement: "The blessings of liberal democracies are too often overestimated, especially by those who have never experienced life without social or economic privilege in their own regime." For many, the blessings of liberal democracy seem both desirable and distressingly elusive. Half a century after the civil rights movement, Martin Luther King Jr. has countless highways named after him, but being Black or brown still dramatically increases your odds of being imprisoned or killed by the police, redlined out of a neighborhood, or shunted into subprime, still-segregated educational institutions. Meanwhile, rich parents compete to pay $50,000 a year to send their children to private "Baby Ivy" kindergartens.

Equal protection on paper means little for those who have suffered sexual violence and who watch offenders get a pass—or to victims of gender bias and discrimination, who see workplace harassers promoted or handed exorbitant exit packages, as often happens at major corporations. Similarly, liberal democracy leaves much to be desired for people whose communities double as environmental sacrifice zones, forcing residents to drink poisoned water and breathe polluted air—while the Environmental Protection Agency rolls back already limited safeguards and standards. Economic democracy feels like a dead letter for the members of an increasingly casualized and debt-ravaged workforce, who can be found holding multiple jobs, driving Uber late into the night after teaching public school by day, or frantically laboring and risking their health in Amazon warehouses to further enrich Jeff Bezos, the wealthiest man on Earth.

During the conference's question-and-answer period, one might have thought Lennard and I had called for the reopening of work camps. Instead, all we did was praise the idea of the Green New Deal—a proposal that purposely pays tribute to the legacy of one of history's most influential liberals, President Franklin Delano Roosevelt—while pointing out that it had taken the arrival of a young and unapologetic democratic socialist,

Representative Ocasio-Cortez, to propose solutions proportional to the ecological catastrophe at hand. Lennard, to her credit, noted that liberals tend to be on the right side of history when difficult battles are comfortably in the past. And she also went out of her way to praise liberal rights frameworks as necessary tools, "insufficient shields and blunt weapons" though they may be. If liberal democracy is incapable of delivering the basic conditions required for democratic participation—"being alive on a not-dead planet, not in a cage, enfranchised, not starving and sick"—then it is our duty, she argued, to question such a system and to challenge it.

Plattner shook his head. "Socialism . . . doesn't strike me as a new idea or a promising idea," he said, flabbergasted. "I'm not used to hearing arguments that question the worth of liberal democracy." Multiple respondents thought it fitting to mention that the German left had helped usher in Hitler, implying that Lennard and I were unwitting handmaidens of totalitarianism. One speaker elicited cheers with an emotional appeal: We should all stand "shoulder to shoulder" to fight Trump, leftists locking arms with neoconservatives to return us to the twentieth-century status quo. Part of me was sympathetic to his call—Trump is, of course, an abomination. But sitting up there next to Bill Kristol, and thinking about how his beloved war on terror had led to the displacement and suffering of the Afghan and Syrian refugees featured in my documentary, and how candidate turned reality TV star Palin had paved the way for reality TV star turned candidate Trump, I couldn't bring myself to clap for a resistance that refused to engage in even minimal political introspection or reassessment.

* * *

Even as many liberals remain skeptical of, or hostile to, the seeming socialist turn in US politics, the right-wing media has been crying wolf about socialism since Fox News was a glimmer in Rupert Murdoch's eye. These conservative appa-ratchiks know what socialism is and aren't afraid to say it: a fifteen-dollar-an-hour minimum wage, paid maternity leave, free college, universal health care, well-paved roads, subsi-dized housing, public television, and so on. The Green New Deal is definitely socialism: "It's a watermelon: green on the outside and deep, deep communist red on the inside," conserv-ative talking head and former Trump adviser Sebastian Gorka intoned from the stage at the February 2019 Conservative Political Action Conference.

Indeed, the growing popularity of socialism may spring at least in part from the longer-term failures of this negative-branding campaign: tell enough people struggling to make ends meet that socialism will allow them to consult a doctor without fear of bankruptcy and perhaps to enjoy a restorative paid vaca-tion now and then, and some are bound to think it sounds like a pretty good idea. That is definitely the gist of a well-traveled social media meme that features an image from a Fox News segment on Ocasio-Cortez, Tlaib, Ilhan Omar, and the other left-aligned lawmakers sworn in to the 116th Congress; it coun-terposes sweetly smiling headshots of the alleged socialist insur-gents alongside bullet-pointed policy goals, such as free college and Medicare for All, that actually poll quite well according to opinion surveys. The graphic makes socialism seem not only ap-pealing, but also au courant, thus inadvertently chipping away at decades of carefully crafted propaganda.

Since 1989, political and cultural elites have worked hard to depict socialism as an outdated and stultifying relic—as state oppression and unfreedom in service of a naive and dangerous fantasy of equality. But as thirty-two-year-old Lee Carter, the lone democratic socialist representative in the Virginia state legislature, tells film director Yael Bridge in *The Big Scary "S" Word*, Cold War fearmongering just doesn't work the way it used to. For a generation understandably worried that they will never find dignified and fairly remunerated work (let alone muster the savings required to own a home or retire), who watch the principal on their high-interest college loans balloon despite regular payments, who have seen extreme weather events and temperature records broken every year of their lives, and who endured an incompetent and cruel government response to a deadly pandemic, the status quo seems untenable. By contrast, the horror of a defunct Soviet bloc seems a far more distant threat than the current dystopia of billionaires seeking to found private space colonies while most of humanity lives in squalor. Youthful converts to left-wing politics may not know exactly what policies democratic socialism would consist of, from the nitty-gritty details of participatory decision-making structures to the role of markets in a world where capital no longer rules. But they do have a sense of what socialism would *feel* like. Socialism would feel like having a future.

Yet today's warning signs of elite institutional collapse in the political mainstream serve chiefly to remind us that socialism's increasing credibility is largely attributable to factors external to any independent mobilization of socialist politics. They mostly stem from a combination of capitalism's failures and conservative overreach rather than from any newfound reserve of strength, savvy, or strategic genius on the left. Read any article in the left press aimed at rousing the socialist faithful, and chances are the final paragraph concludes with some variation of "we have a world to win." But in my more cynical or anxious moments, I'm tempted to say the opposite: the left has a world to lose—or rather, a promising shift in the political winds to squander or blow.

The signs that people, particularly people under forty, are more open to socialist politics than they have been in generations are remarkable and encouraging, but they also pose the problem of collective self-definition. The left—whatever exactly the "left" in the United States is—must rise to, and seize, the occasion. The largest challenge ahead is to move socialism from the fringe to the center of political life and turn people into committed democratic socialists—as opposed to people who tell pollsters they prefer socialism to capitalism or that Bernie Sanders was their favorite candidate in the ring. (During the 2020 Democratic primary most of these same poll respondents also reported that centrist Joe Biden, and not the more left-leaning Elizabeth Warren, was their second choice, thus calling the ideological coherence of their proclivities into serious doubt.)

This is a momentous task and a tall order for any movement, let alone one mostly made up of people who are new to activism. Through no fault of their own, young people have come of age in a sort of political vacuum and in a society that extends precious few opportunities for democratic engagement beyond the ballot box. In the blasted political landscape facing most millennial socialists today, few organizations exist to pass on institutional memory and hard-won knowledge about the ins and outs and ups and downs of organizing. (Labor unions, invaluable though they may be, are beleaguered and shrinking.) To build a mass base, any viable socialist movement must be as welcoming as possible to all comers, no matter how inexperienced or uncool. It must be generous and patient while also being strategically disciplined and tough-minded.

These challenges are formidable, and may well sink the socialist ship before it ever really sets sail. (The intense opposition and corporate sabotage that would be unleashed should the vessel ever gain real momentum are also important to consider, though beyond our purview here.) Yet people are already making progress, and every bit counts. If we look at the left as a whole—as opposed to zooming in to focus on the inevitable internecine and interpersonal squabbles—the situation today remains far more promising than it was at the start of the last decade. Then, in the wake of the worst global recession since the 1930s, the people shouting the loudest about financial injustice were racist, incoherent Tea Party disciples. Now, in contrast, the left has a prominent voice in the national conversation about economics, thanks to a combination of theory and practice: a journalistic boom in socialist commentary that spread from independent magazines such as *Jacobin*, *n+1*, *Viewpoint*, and *Current Affairs* to more mainstream channels; a steady stream of grassroots mobilizations, from Occupy Wall Street to Black Lives Matter to a wave of strikes led by teachers, debtors, feminists, and concerned kids to rescue the planet from climate catastrophe; and the election of socialists to local, state, and national office.

People are learning in real time. In 2011, the Occupy movement reflected the then-dominant tendency on the activist left—or at least the predominantly white and anarchist left—

of rejecting any attempt to exercise or take power. Occupy participants (myself among them) resisted many pragmatic appeals to recognize leadership, collaborate with labor unions, make specific demands of the state, or join electoral campaigns. That skepticism isn't totally gone—and it can be healthy in properly administered doses—but today's left activists have reassessed it and rightly found it lacking. A new generation is rejecting the old equation, long common in radical circles, holding that group discipline is a form of domination, that losing is a sign of political purity, and that change can only come from outside—even if we also know socialism will never be won solely at the voting booth. If nothing else, explicitly orienting a movement as socialist requires the recognition of two things: first, the central role of class conflict in our society, reminding us that laborers, not bosses or investors, are the principal source of economic and social value; and second, the significance of the state as the repository of a crucial set of publicly accountable institutions that should come under people's control and, eventually, be transformed to serve people's genuine interests in the process.

In contrast to conservatives, with their clear vision of what this socialist transformation would entail—an oppressive nanny state smothering its citizens with free checkups and child care—avowed socialists are far less likely to be confident about what lies ahead. "There is no model we can point to. We have no idea what it would be like to live in a society free of exploitation and how that would change people," Keeanga-Yamahtta Taylor, a prominent socialist and expert on race and housing policy, told me.

Democratic socialism, after all, cannot simply be more robust public services or more stringently regulated markets—however nice free checkups and child care may be. Such reforms are the hallmarks of *social democracy*, the fragile compact between capitalism and the welfare state now coming undone even in its Scandinavian and Canadian strongholds. Since democratic socialism has never been tried at scale, no one knows precisely what it would involve, or how it could be brought about. Indeed, as Michael Harrington, a founder of the newly reinvigorated Democratic Socialists of America, wrote in 1989 toward the end of his life, "One of the main consequences of the socialist movement has been not socialism but a more humane, rational, and intelligent capitalism." That's undeniably a good thing, Harrington explained, but he also cautioned that many past efforts to implement socialism had been more ambiguous, "sometimes disastrously wrong or else vague and merely rhetorical."

Under capitalism, the power of capital, of money and markets, dominates. This is the current reality we all live and breathe. But what would change if social power—which is the heart of socialism, after all—set society's course? Such an arrangement would be a far cry from the authoritarian, bureaucratic collectivism, or statism, that collapsed at the end of the last century. (Though policy-minded democratic socialists should by all means build on examples and lessons from the other socialist experiments long overshadowed by the Soviet Union, looking at, say, health care and organic agriculture in Cuba; educational policies in Kerala, India; the short-lived attempt to build distributed or "cybernetic" decision-making technology in Chile; and the workplace cooperatives of the former Yugoslavia.) The challenge, however, as Harrington himself observed, is that while Marx "assumed that 'society' would take over direction of the economy from the capitalists . . . there is no unitary subject of historic action called 'society.'" And this analytical absence opens, in turn, onto a host of real-world political dilemmas.

* * *

During a recent visit to Saint Petersburg, Florida, I overheard a group of activists discussing tenant organizing and gentrification at a local coffee shop. Some wore pins and T-shirts associated with the Dream Defenders, a racial and economic justice group founded soon after Trayvon Martin was murdered by George Zimmerman—a man whose right to "stand his ground" and shoot perceived threatening figures at will was deemed more salient than Martin's right to live. When I asked if they saw any signs of socialism's growing popularity in their day-to-day organizing efforts, they looked at me as if I was a cop or a crazy person. After duly consulting Google, they accepted my explanation that I was in town showing a film at a nearby campus.

It would have hardly mattered if I was a narc, however, since they didn't have much to report. Sure, there has been an uptick in antiestablishment sentiment since 2016, they told me—but they also all agreed it was the kind of energy that could go either way, funneled to the left or right, depending on what explanatory frameworks and movements people encountered first. Socialists, in other words, aren't born but made—and the left's capacity for outreach, in central Florida as in most areas, is profoundly limited.

"I am a socialist," one person responded when I asked outright, but they added a qualification—they identified with Black socialism, a tradition that runs from W. E. B. Du Bois through the Black Panthers, not the sort of socialism that's broadly identified with Bernie Sanders. They'd experienced too much discrimination from white people of all income levels to believe that racism could be eradicated by focusing on class politics alone, and they felt that too many lefty neophytes believed that to be the case. When I asked what Black socialism meant, I got an answer both concise and moving: freedom. "Freedom not just to live but thrive, to love who I want to love, to not have to work a soul-crushing job, to be free, but not the kind of freedom that depends on dominating others."

As I got up to leave, a young man who had been listening finally weighed in. On his computer, he drew up an old map of Saint Petersburg from the 1930s, which vividly showed the less desirable, redlined areas where the community's Black residents were forced to live, a place he grew up in and still called home. "I'm frustrated by the whole conversation about socialism versus capitalism, as though they are separate things," he said. The current and disproportionate affluence that white communities possess, he explained, has been built on centuries of state intervention and assistance: Military forces stole Indigenous land, the government parceled it out and gave it away to white farmers, and then a whole apparatus of development and finance was mobilized, first to exclude Black people, and then bringing them back within limited reach of credit and capital—but only on the lending industry's predatory terms. The New Deal and postwar systems of government-enabled prosperity and worker rights instrumental in elevating the white, suburban middle class shut out swaths of the citizenry. As a result, in 2019 the median wealth of white families in the United States hovered at around $188,000, compared with the $24,000 possessed by their Black counterparts.

The beneficiaries of racialized access to capital also enjoy the priceless bonus of socially sanctioned self-deception: they get to believe that their wealth was earned on the "free market," the product of hard work and a pristine frontier-style capitalism untainted by welfare or socialism. None of this, of course, could be further from the truth. Middle- and upper-class white people aren't forced to acknowledge and feel guilty for the public benefits they receive, while poor mothers are made to feel ashamed for using food stamps to feed their kids.

Socialism, the young man argued, already exists; it's just not evenly distributed. Various government programs like tax breaks (from mortgage-interest deductions to claimed depreciations in commercial ventures) are designed to support the already privileged indirectly and imperceptibly. Meanwhile, aid to the poor is direct and demeaning (you can't spell *means-tested* without *mean*). At the same time, research shows that many Americans who receive direct federal benefits, including Medicare and Social Security, wrongly report that they have never received government aid—perhaps because these are services they feel they have paid for, like any other product. The challenge for socialists, then, involves bringing what the political scientist Suzanne Mettler has called the "submerged state" above ground and into the light in order to identify and expand its benefits and beneficiaries, democratize its mechanisms, and decommodify more and more areas of life.

Decommodification is a key element of this process—"There should be no profit motive connected to things that human beings cannot survive without," as Keeanga-Yamahtta Taylor put it when we spoke—and not as radical a move as it may seem. Placing things beyond the market purview is hardly an untested or utopian concept. Public schools, for example, are based on the conviction that education is something everyone is entitled to, regardless of their ability to pay. Countries with universal health care have come to a similar determination about medicine, deciding potentially lifesaving medical treatments should not be limited to those who are wealthy enough to afford them. Every minute of every day, we use infrastructure and access information, from public roads to weather forecasts, that are universal and free. This is why democratic socialists are right to focus, for the time being, on proposals like Medicare for All and free college.

But the question at the center of socialism, Taylor continued, is not what services the state should provide—such as whether or not public housing should be more widely available, or whether there should be a jobs guarantee or a basic income or both—but rather who *owns* the state. "For me, socialism is about the collective control of society by the majority of people," she said. "Right now, the majority of people, the people who create society's wealth, never get asked questions about how society should be run." The US offers a minimal safety net but no opportunity for self-rule; "recipients" of welfare are objects of government assistance, not agents in collective decision-making or self-determination. What services they receive, or are denied, get determined by elected officials in Washington, who tend to be older, white, male millionaires— meaning that they have little insight into the lives of the people they ostensibly represent.

This problem, Taylor said, won't be solved by electing representatives who look more like the constituents they supposedly serve. "People today think the problem is access. They think that we need to remedy exclusions with inclusions. What gets missed is the nature of the institutions people are being integrated into." (James Baldwin, as always, put it best: "Do I really *want* to be integrated into a burning house?") Currently, the affluence and high purchasing power of a few people come at the expense of the insecurity and poverty of many, many more. We're trapped, as Alexandria Ocasio-Cortez has said, in a "scarcity mindset," which posits that a small number can win only when others lose. Freedom, as the activist I met implied, flows from domination. The job of socialists is to convince people—including ourselves—that it doesn't have to be that way. What Engels somewhat melodramatically, but also alluringly, called the "kingdom of freedom" can only be achieved by cooperation, not competition—and by breaking the power of a system that hoards resources and makes it seem as if there's not enough to go around.

Marx once described communism as "the riddle of history solved." It marked, in his view, "the genuine resolution of the conflict between man and nature and between man and man—the true resolution of the strife between existence and essence, between objectification and self-confirmation, between freedom and necessity, between the individual and the species." One of my big fears for the rising left is that its adherents will uncritically sign on to this view of things—holding up the words "democratic socialism" as the solution without recognizing the immensity of the philosophical and pragmatic puzzles those two terms contain.

As I argue at length in my book *Democracy May Not Exist, but We'll Miss It When It's Gone*, even if we managed to close the gap between the rich and the poor, to break down the divisions between owners of capital and the working class, we'd still be awash in political challenges. Each chapter of the book focuses on a paradox, or tension, that I believe is central to the democratic project, and that would persist even if we managed to transcend capitalism. We'd still have to balance local and global concerns, to figure out the right mix of structure and spontaneity, to weigh the needs of people alive now with generations yet to come, to marshal expertise while accounting for mass opinion, and so on. Under a more economically egalitarian, explicitly socialist system, these democratic dilemmas will not disappear. The riddle would not be solved. Instead, our problems would become more interesting.

Right now, we remain trapped in social and political battles that, no matter how high the stakes involved, are both maddening and banal. Should billionaires have the right to ungodly sums accumulated through the immiseration of entire populations and the destruction of the ecosystems on which life as we know it depends? Are women the equals of men, Black and brown people the equals of white people, queer people the equals of straight people, trans and nonbinary people equal to cisgender people, the disabled equal to the able-bodied, and so on? I'm going to go out on a limb and say the answers to these questions should be self-evident, even if settling them will require a power struggle of epic proportions. Should we ever resolve these questions in favor of the abolition of billionaires, the desirability of a healthy and inhabitable planet, and the equality of humankind, countless fascinating questions we don't get to ask within the distressingly retrograde confines of our current political and social order could finally come to the fore.

A partial sampling of such questions would include, but are by no means limited to, the following: How much top-down planning will be required to create an ecologically sustainable economy or just a functional one? And how will markets, money, and finance be democratized and fit into the mix? How should we balance collective ownership of our natural common wealth with local and worker control—and how do we combine local and worker control with the ideal of international solidarity? How are the boundaries of decision-making communities to be determined and accountability to be enforced? When can democracy be direct, when must it be representative, and how could randomness or sortition—selecting people to serve as public officials, as we do with juries, instead of electing them—be put to good use? What incentives will motivate people to do necessary but unpleasant work after greed and fear of destitution are no longer in the driver's seat? When is coercion legitimate, and how will people be given real choice over things that matter (as opposed to, for instance, the false and frustrating choice of multiple overpriced and inadequate health insurance providers)? Should we ever manage to overcome the dominant modes of inequality and exploitation that have long distorted basic living conditions under American capitalism, democratic conundrums more rewarding and thorny than the ones that currently preoccupy us will open up in droves.

Under socialism, we would have to prioritize experimenting—collectively thinking and working these and other challenges through. And under a radically divergent plan of social value, that prospect wouldn't have to be as daunting as it may sound now—because socialist arrangements would not only redistribute prosperity more broadly, but also freely apportion two intangible goods that are now in short supply: trust and time. Democracy, which insists that everyone should have a political voice, cannot manifest itself in the absence of trust, which is now stingily meted out as though it's a scarce and precious resource. Under a socialist economic model, where people work to meet the needs of the community and not to produce excess profits for the boss, free time for both leisure and legislating would increase.

It all sounds terribly utopian—especially when typed on a laptop constructed through an international, exploitative, and extractive supply chain. Staring at my computer, and imagining the complex networks of human beings and logistics that got it to my desk, I'm reminded of a footnote in *Memoirs of a Revolutionist*, a chronicle by the essayist Dwight MacDonald, who briefly flirted with revolutionary politics in the 1930s and '40s. "I remember once walking in the street and suddenly really *seeing* the big heavy buildings in their obstinate actuality and realizing I simply couldn't imagine all this recalcitrant matter transformed by socialism," he writes. "How would the street *look* when the workers took it over, how could revolution transfigure the miles and miles of stubborn stone? I couldn't conceive of a flame hot enough to melt into new forms this vast solid Is." Sometimes, while I'm gazing up at an urban skyline or sitting at home typing on my keyboard, his rumination pops into my mind, and I feel ridiculous to have ever entertained the idea that our economy and society could be remade.

At least that's what I *thought* MacDonald said. Recently I picked up the book and realized I had not retained the second half of his recollection: "A few years later, bombing fleets did melt away great sections of the world's cities and the political structure of many nations was pulverized," he says. The passage continued on the following page. The buildings, and the social order they represented, were not so immutable after all.

Today the searing heat may not come from bomber planes, but from climate change, from rising temperatures and forest fires—and the melting may be of ice caps, swallowing our coastal cities from the bottom up or flooding our towns and farmlands. Billions of humans may eventually be refugees from climate change; nonhuman species that once graced our Earth will cease to be; billionaires will become trillionaires, and maybe some will escape to New Zealand, to the moon, or to Mars. The world is changing, whether we like it or not. And as we face that crucial fact, we might as well try to change it for the better, by fighting to ensure that more of us have a chance to enjoy the blessings that liberal democracy promised, but also by refusing to abandon the possibility that even more satisfying, sustainable, and dignified forms of life might lie ahead.

6

OUT WITH THE OLD

In the United States, democracy is dominated by the old. In 2020, a shambolic Donald Trump, seventy-four, faced off against three septuagenarian Democratic Party challengers. Joe Biden, seventy-eight, triumphed at the polls, making him the oldest president in the nation's history. But the problem isn't limited to a senescent head of state. The average senator is now almost sixty-three and the average member of the House nearly fifty-eight, making them roughly twenty years older than their average constituent, and nearly a decade older than their counterparts were in 1981.

Older people today hold disproportionate power because they have the numbers and the means to do so. People sixty-five and older, for example, are more than three times as likely to make political donations as those under thirty. As a result, their voices, amplified by money, carry farther politically than those of the young and impecunious.

There are a lot of voices in their chorus. The United States electorate is the oldest it's been since at least 1970 and is gray-

_____

* Previously published as "Out With the Old, In With the Young," *New York Times*, October 18, 2019.

ing at a rapid clip, with the well-off living longer than ever before. By 2034, according to the Census Bureau, the population sixty-five and older will exceed the population under eighteen; by 2060 the sixty-five-and-older crowd is projected to have almost doubled. There are some seventy-four million baby boomers alone, and when election time comes, they turn out in droves. During the 2018 midterms, 64 percent of citizens ages fifty-four to seventy-two cast a ballot, compared to 31 percent of eligible voters ages twenty-nine and under.

"Money, numbers and power have been inexorably accruing to the aging 'baby boomer' generation for the last few decades," the political scientist John Seery warned in his 2011 book, *Too Young to Run?* The trends show no signs of slowing. Migration to metropolitan centers by people who tend to be younger and more diverse, along with rural depopulation and aging, will only intensify age-based inequities given the geographic biases of the American electoral system. Call it the coming gerontocracy.

While significant divisions exist *within* every age cohort (many older people in this country are progressive and poor, just as some young people are rich and right-wing), the divisions *between* older and younger generations are becoming increasingly salient. Of course, young people are not intrinsically enlightened or virtuous compared to their elders—I certainly hope that's not the case—and our society desperately needs older people to participate in public life.

But our democracy is in a moment of crisis. People are, for good reason, losing faith in institutions, parties, and political processes and questioning long-standing assumptions. Everything, it seems, is up for grabs. The lack of intergenerational justice, of equity between the young and old, is an underappreciated facet of the current turmoil: a hoary establishment hoards influence, curtailing young people's ability to effect change.

That is not to say that the faults in America's political system are solely the result of its biases against the young. The problems we face are myriad, and addressing gerontocracy won't solve them all. But an antiquated system that produces unrepresentative leadership is ill equipped to respond to the problems of our time. And that should concern anyone committed to democratic ideals.

A profound and growing experiential divide now fuels conflicting outlooks, material interests, and political priorities. Not only is the cohort of people born after 1980 much more diverse than that of Americans now entering retirement (nearly 80 percent of Americans over sixty-five are white, a figure that drops to around 50 percent for people between six and twenty-one) but they were also less well-off compared to their predecessors at the same age. (Given the persistence of racial discrimination, though, diversity and precarity cannot be neatly disentangled.)

Contrary to stereotypes, polls show that young people across the political spectrum are deeply concerned about the state of the world. This concern has translated into rising youth voter turnout and a resurgence of protest movements. On a range of issues, including global warming, gun control, economic inequality, racism, immigration, and trans rights, youth-led movements are creating a generational insurgency.

But this insurgency faces major obstacles. From age limits on voting and eligibility for office to the way House districts are drawn to the problem of money in politics, our modern political system is stacked against the young. These barriers need to be openly acknowledged and broken down.

* * *

Black and Indigenous people, white men without property, women, and some religious groups were all excluded from America's original democratic compact. So were young people, though we rarely consider this fact.

In *Too Young to Run?* Professor Seery argues that the Constitution effectively treats young people as second-class citizens by imposing minimum age requirements for elected federal office: twenty-five for Congress, thirty for the Senate, and thirty-five for president. The nation's framers, the youngest of whom was twenty-six, Seery writes, "Bequeathed an age bias unto posterity by which they themselves did not fully abide," devising rules ensuring that the country would be governed by people more senior than themselves. The founders no doubt knew that *senex*, a Latin root of the word *senator*, means "old man."

The geographically based idiosyncrasies of American democracy that the founders put in place compound the problem. On average, ballots cast by older people hold more weight and are less frequently "wasted" than those of the young. (Wasted votes are those garnered in excess of what a candidate needs to win; in our winner-take-all systems that means anything over 50 percent.) Clustered in sparsely populated states and counties, voters who are older, whiter, and wealthier get a boost: older Americans wield disproportionate sway over the Electoral College, the Senate, and a gerrymandered Congress.

Migration patterns worsen these trends. A growing percentage of young people now dream of city life, but their preferences inadvertently reduce their political clout: "18 percent of rural residents are 65 or older vs. 15 percent in suburban and small metro counties and 13 percent in cities," the Pew Research Center reported in 2018. Millennials, concentrated in metropolitan areas, are the predominant generation of potential voters in only 86 congressional districts, while boomer voters predominate in 341. By 2040, 70 percent of Americans are expected to live in the fifteen most populous states. That would mean that 70 percent of America will be represented by only thirty senators.

* * *

In the fall of 2019, millions of people around the world took to the streets as part of the youth-led Global Climate Strike, a week of protests timed with the United Nations climate summit. The movement began when a Swedish teenager named Greta Thunberg stopped attending classes to protest government failure to curb greenhouse gas emissions. Thunberg said she was inspired by the anti-gun-violence walkouts led by high school students from Parkland, Florida.

One person who took up Thunberg's call to action was Haven Coleman, a thirteen-year-old from Colorado. A cofounder of the national group US Youth Climate Strike, she began skipping school every Friday to head to the steps of the state capitol in Denver. Older people would often stop to tell her they didn't understand why she was protesting. "Because you didn't do it," she'd reply.

The environment is one of the critical lines separating the old from the young. Baby boomers may have helped organize the first Earth Day in 1970, but back then ecological disaster was a more distant threat. Today, intimate knowledge of planetary devastation, from hurricanes to forest fires, is distressingly common. When the Colorado hills burn, Coleman's asthma flares up.

The other critical divide is the economy. The boomers who came of age in the 1950s and '60s benefited from boom times while millennials and Generation Z have been dogged by the aftermath of the mortgage meltdown, Gilded Age levels of inequality, and a recession triggered by Covid-19, which caused youth unemployment to disproportionately spike. One generation enjoyed a comparatively high minimum wage, affordable college tuition, and reasonable costs of living. For every one after, stagnating wages, ballooning student debt, and unaffordable housing have become the norm.

"Millennials are less well off than members of earlier generations when they were young," a 2018 report by economists from the Federal Reserve Board bluntly states. Other economists have shown that a household headed by someone born in 1970 has a quarter less income and 40 percent less wealth than one headed by a comparable person born in 1940. In contrast, between 1989 and 2013, only the cohort of families headed by people at least sixty-two years of age saw an increase in median wealth. Older people are more likely to own property, stocks, and other assets—and, consequently, to prefer policies that will keep the values of those assets high. No wonder so many young people have pivoted left, rejecting conventional wisdom about the virtues of unfettered capitalism.

Just as affluence translates into political power, being comparatively precarious creates a disempowering feedback loop. Burdened by student loans, young people are postponing home ownership, marriage, and starting families. As a result, they are less likely to feel they have a stake in the communities where they live, which means they are less likely to participate politically and thus have their interests adequately represented. This puts policies overwhelmingly favored by the young at a further disadvantage.

*　*　*

Some might argue that the problem of gerontocracy isn't really a problem at all. Even if young people do not have equal political rights as older people, it evens out eventually; young people actually do possess the same political rights as their elders, just not yet.

The limits of this "be patient and wait your turn" attitude were on display when protesters associated with the youth-led Sunrise Movement clashed with Senator Dianne Feinstein of California, then eighty-five, over the need for a Green New Deal. In a video of the encounter, a group ranging in age from eleven to twenty-four insist that Feinstein is duty bound to listen to their concerns about the warning by the Intergovernmental Panel on Climate Change that we have just over a decade to avert the worst effects of global warming. "Well, you didn't vote for me," the senator says, dismissing a girl who says she is sixteen.

For any adult with half a conscience, the senator's remarks held up a discomfiting mirror, a reminder of our complicity in the present crisis. For younger viewers, it encapsulated a growing sense that many older people, even those who are ostensibly liberals, are dangerously blasé about the future—and that their willingness to play with fire stems from their belief that they won't live long enough to get burned.

A month after the confrontation with Feinstein went viral, getting more than ten million views, Representative Ayanna Pressley of Massachusetts introduced a proposal to lower the federal voting age to sixteen. Since the era of Plato's *Republic*, aged-based exclusions have almost always been justified in terms of youthful immaturity and the wisdom that comes with experience. Pressley instead highlighted the fact that young people have their own distinct experiential wisdom:

> A sixteen-year-old will bring with them the 2019 fears that their father's insulin will run out before the next paycheck.

> A seventeen-year-old will bring with them the 2019 hopes to be the first in their family to earn a college degree.

> A seventeen-year-old will bring with them a 2019 solemn vow to honor the lives of their classmates stolen by a gunman.

The proposal failed by 126 to 305, an outcome in line with the likely result if the matter were put to a popular vote: A full 75 percent of registered voters oppose enfranchising seventeen-year-olds; 84 percent oppose it for sixteen-year-olds. (Individual states, however, may lower the voting age for state and local elections.)

David Runciman, a professor of politics at Cambridge, disagrees with mainstream public sentiment. The structural disenfranchisement of young people, he argues, must be remedied by even more drastic measures. His proposal: enfranchise everyone over the age of six. "What's the worst that could happen?" he asked on a podcast last year. Given the disturbing characters that have been elected to high office around the world, including Narendra Modi and Donald Trump, it's not clear that letting kids vote would yield worse outcomes than what adults have delivered.

For Professor Runciman, the fundamental issue is fairness. He points to the 2016 Brexit vote, in which 73 percent of the 18–24 age group cast a ballot for Remain when more than 60 percent of 65 and older voted Leave. Hundreds of thousands of people who were too young to vote will have to spend their entire lives dealing with the repercussions of a nostalgic, ill-considered decision made by people not long for this earth.

It turns out there are plenty of pragmatic reasons to lower the voting age, if not to six then to sixteen. And not just because politicians like Senator Feinstein would have to listen to kids about global warming.

In 2013, Takoma Park, Maryland, became the first city in the United States to lower the voting age for local elections to sixteen. The turnout rate of sixteen- and seventeen-year-olds in the next election was nearly twice that of those eighteen and older, inspiring the nearby town of Hyattsville to follow Takoma Park's example.

Something similar happened in local elections in Norway in 2011, when twenty-one municipalities conducted a trial lowering the voting age from eighteen to sixteen. A range of studies support the conclusion that eighteen is not the optimal age to bestow the right to vote. People are leaving the nest and too preoccupied navigating college and work to figure out how to cast a ballot, let alone register to do so.

It is also the case that voting, though typically regarded as the paramount individual right, is actually a social affair. Research conducted in Denmark shows that having children old enough to vote at home makes their parents more likely to vote as well. And it's habitual: once you vote, you are more likely to do it again. A person's first election is critical, a kind of democratic gateway drug, and it's best to get them hooked young.

Sixteen seems a reasonable time to start. And lowering the voting age might also encourage more young people to run in the local and state races where the Constitution's age restrictions do not apply.

* * *

If our goal is to break the grip of the coming gerontocracy, giving more teenagers access to the ballot is a necessary but insufficient step. The inequities that result from the role of money in politics and our geographically based electoral system also need to be remedied. Otherwise, the power structure will keep pandering to older—and whiter and more affluent—voters.

To approach something resembling intergenerational justice, at least two additional transformations are required: campaign finance reform and a more proportional system of representation.

The imbalance of financial resources between the young and the old puts a generational twist on a long-standing conundrum: the concentration of political power that flows from concentration of wealth is anathema to the principle of political equality. A teenager working for minimum wage or a young parent struggling with student debt should have the same influence over her elected representatives as a retiree who has amassed a lifetime of wealth. Publicly financing elections would go a long way toward putting people of different ages on more even political footing.

At the same time, we need a new motto. Not "One person, one vote," but "One person, one equally meaningful vote." The 2019 Fair Representation Act proposed in the House is a step in the right direction, pointing the way to a more proportional model of congressional representation using larger multi-member districts. (The imbalances inherent to the Senate and Electoral College would need to be fixed through other means.)

Under a proportional system, if a party wins the support of 25 percent of votes cast by a given electorate, it gets 25 percent of the seats—votes are no longer "wasted," and more people are represented. Research indicates that more proportional systems may increase youth turnout by as much as 12 percentage points while also encouraging younger candidates to run for office. Larger districts would help address the problem of gerrymandering while urban-rural polarization, and the age-based inequities that stem from it, would diminish.

Some might respond that pursuing generational parity is the wrong approach. Recently, Oxford University professor William MacAskill proposed age-weighting votes in favor of the young. By his accounting, eighteen- to twenty-seven-year-olds should possess six times the voting weight of someone sixty-eight or older. Whether desirable or not, his thought experiment is provocative: Why shouldn't those who will have to live longer with the consequences of elections have more of a say?

Such imaginative reforms are, of course, distant and unlikely prospects, which means it is incumbent on older people to find more immediate ways to express intergenerational solidarity. Just as many men stand against patriarchy, so can older people resist the gerontocracy.

Unlike their boomer predecessors who rallied under the ageist motto "Don't trust anyone over thirty," kids today are eager to find venerable allies. Consider the popularity of the seventy-eight-year-old democratic socialist Bernie Sanders or the fact that the seventy-three-year-old senator Ed Markey (a cosponsor, along with Representative Alexandria Ocasio-Cortez, of the Green New Deal) secured the endorsement of the youthful Sunrise Movement over his telegenic thirty-nine-year-old primary challenger. They may be septuagenarians, but they embrace millennial priorities.

Those of us who are older, if not wiser, should take another cue from young activists. We need to support forward-looking policies, and we also need to protest.

On October 11, 2019, several thousand people, including Thunberg, gathered near the Colorado capitol. For once, Coleman wasn't the only climate striker in sight. Addressing the crowd, she didn't spend a moment pleading to be formally enfranchised (though she has told me she thinks sixteen-year-olds should be). Her overwhelming mission was to spur adults to join the revolt. "Our hard work does not absolve you of action," she said. "Adults, step up."

Coleman's emphasis on the power of protest is historically informed. If the past proves anything, it is that structural reforms are rarely secured through elections alone. We should see the goal of including young people in political life as part of the prolonged fight for a more robust and inclusive democracy—a system, lest we forget, based on the premise that those affected by a decision should have a say in making it. This task is all the more urgent given the concerted effort to undermine hard-won democratic gains. The generational implications of brazen attempts to shore up minority rule by shrinking and disempowering the electorate through methods such as gerrymandering, voter ID laws, and dark money too often go unremarked.

In 1776, John Adams wrote that the legislature should be in miniature "an exact portrait of the people at large—it should think, feel, reason and act like them." Should we ever build a movement powerful enough to create a government that takes this founder at his word, the result could be astounding: a democracy in which elected officials are responsive to the full range of their constituents; universal access to college and medical care ensuring an educated and healthy citizenry; and the environment protected for generations to come. Over the long term, these outcomes—and this more democratic system—would benefit the vast majority of people, young and old alike.

7

THE END
OF THE UNIVERSITY

In the spring of 2020, I began taking walks around the University of North Carolina's Greensboro campus, where my father works as a professor of chemistry. Soon after I arrived down South, classes moved online and the vast majority of students decamped for home. The spacious campus turned desolate, bicycles locked up everywhere as though the people who rode them had vaporized. For months little changed, with the exception of a large boulder that sits near the main green and serves as a kind of community billboard. In the beginning, the message spray-painted on it was hopeful: "Wash your hands so we can graduate," the artist implored. In a matter of weeks, it grew resigned: "COVID-19," the rock read, "Class of 2020." By early June it was rebellious: "George," "Ahmaud," "Breonna," "Black Lives Matter."

What is going to happen to universities moving forward and to their students, faculty, and staff—not to mention the

---

* Previously published as "The End of the University: The Pandemic Should Force America to Remake Higher Education," *New Republic*, September 8, 2020.

surrounding communities and businesses that depend on campus life to stay afloat? No one knows, but everyone agrees the situation is dire. Some state systems forecasted losses of up to a billion dollars by the end of 2020. The virus sparked a national conversation about the value of education. Scrambling to adapt to online teaching often creates more work for faculty with less payoff for students isolated from their teachers and peers. Across the country, including at the University of North Carolina, students filed suits to get tuition refunds, on the grounds they were denied the "true college experience," and signed petitions demanding that their housing costs be reimbursed. In March, Moody's downgraded the sector's outlook from stable to negative, citing the prospect of reduced enrollment. With universities and colleges in desperate need of funds far in excess of the $14 billion in federal stimulus money allotted by the CARES Act, Covid-19 may well be what some have called an "extinction-level event" for higher education. Schools often run deficits in normal times; in 2019 nearly one thousand private colleges were already borderline insolvent. Covid will cause many to shutter for good. It is accounting, not epidemiology, that drives so many university administrators to push for a rapid return to business as usual, effectively demanding that faculty and staff sacrifice their lives for the financial health of their employer. In August, UNC officials brazenly invited students to move back into their dorms for fall semester. In a little more than a week the system's flagship school, UNC–Chapel Hill, pivoted to remote instruction after multiple outbreak clusters emerged. I, for one, encouraged my father to resist the pressure to return to the classroom on a rushed and reckless timeline.

Walking around the ghostly Greensboro campus that summer, it felt like I'd arrived in the future that highly paid tech pundits have long claimed was inevitable—a dystopia where instruction takes place solely online and traditional college is obsolete. The people invested in digital disruption are not alone in their push to end higher education as we know it. North Carolina may have been the first state to establish a functioning public university back in 1795, but Republican legislators—so keen on southern heritage when a Confederate monument is at stake—have been working for years to dismantle the state's educational legacy, slashing appropriations while targeting specific academic initiatives (including an antipoverty law program and one focused on biodiversity). Convinced colleges are hotbeds of liberal political correctness, they are eager to see lecture halls, libraries, and laboratories close for good.

Democrats, too, facilitated higher education's evisceration; they bear substantial responsibility for public institutions being so uniquely, and unnecessarily, vulnerable to the pandemic's fiscal shock. For decades, disinvestment in higher education has been a bipartisan undertaking. Looming state budget deficits and austerity policies ensure that even more schools will be public in name alone. Cuts, unfortunately, tend to stick: after the 2008 crash, state funding for higher education never rebounded. Even before Covid, state higher-ed spending, on average, was down around 17 percent per student, adjusted for inflation, from pre-recession levels. Meanwhile, the market-friendly fixes adopted over the years to make up for declining state revenue—a growing dependence on tuition dollars and proceeds from real estate holdings, athletics, and hospitals—have recently been exposed as massive liabilities, as vacant dormitories, stadiums, and surgery wards collect not income but dust. Donors, who in good times might be inclined to give generously to an endowment in exchange for a tax break and a plaque, may prefer now to tighten their belts.

Of course, those schools that aren't rich enough to have medical complexes and endowments will be hardest hit. In the most likely scenario, the comparatively privileged will compete ever more frantically for space in academia's upper echelons, while millions of poor and working-class students, disproportionately Black and brown, are funneled into dilapidated community colleges and for-profit degree mills or give up on studying altogether. Harvard and Yale will not just survive this calamity; they will likely see their stock rise. Princeton's $26 billion endowment generates about $158,000 in annual revenue for each of its approximately 8,200 students. In contrast, the nation's historically Black colleges and universities, which lack comparable cash reserves, will be especially harmed by closures.

Before UNC students were called back for an uncertain and perilous fall semester, I often felt sentimental. Crossing the abandoned quad or passing the lonely statue of Minerva, I missed the usual hustle and bustle and wistfully regarded the signs of devotion to scholarship and learning. And yet, as someone who had spent the previous eight years campaigning to end student debt and advance the demand for tuition-free, and intellectually freeing, public college for all, I knew the university must not be romanticized. The question is not whether the university as it currently exists will survive the pandemic, but whether we want it to.

The coronavirus pandemic did not deliver an unexpected blow to an otherwise healthy patient; it exposed and exacerbated an array of preexisting conditions, revealing structural inequalities that go back not just decades but centuries. Capitalist imperatives and racial exclusions have distorted and damaged our education system since its inception. The country's universities were built on a corrupt foundation: the theft of Indigenous territory and the owning and leasing of enslaved people provided much of the initial acreage, labor, and capital for many of the country's most esteemed institutions. President Abraham Lincoln signed the Morrill Act in 1862, the year before the Emancipation Proclamation, handing over millions of acres of stolen land to found universities, which shut out Black people with few exceptions. The Morrill Act was part of a concerted effort to modernize the economy. Indeed, the research university and the business corporation developed in tandem. Racism, commerce, and education have been bedfellows from the beginning. If we want a real cure for the crisis, we must change how our institutions of learning are funded and governed, so that they might embody a deeper, democratic purpose at long last.

The root of the word *apocalypse* literally means to uncover or unveil. Destruction doesn't have to be the only outcome. Difficult revelations can also be a spur to insight and action. Increasingly stratified, segregated, and costly access to higher education is not the only possible future we are racing toward, but it is the default—the destination that aligns with our past and present trajectories. In order to forge another path, we must engage in a deeper form of accounting. Beyond finding a way to balance university budgets in the midst of global depression, the challenge is to acknowledge and repair ongoing inequities, thereby making our higher-education system, for the first time in our troubled history, truly public. If our goal is to shift course and avert the disaster on the horizon, the boulder's final message—"Black Lives Matter"—points us in the right direction. "If Black women were free, it would mean that everyone else would have to be free since our freedom would necessitate the destruction of all the systems of oppression," the Combahee River Collective, an influential group of Black feminists, wrote in 1977. Their wisdom still holds. If we could create a world where Black students were free to learn at free universities, we would have created a world where everyone else was finally able to do so as well.

* * *

In 2014, the Debt Collective launched the country's first student debt strike, helping to win more than a billion dollars of debt relief for tens of thousands of people who had attended predatory for-profit colleges. My collaborators and I have been agitating for full student debt abolition and free college ever since, pointing to research that shows that canceling all $1.7 trillion of student debt would provide an economic stimulus of up to $108 billion a year, freeing money currently sent to loan servicers to be spent on other things, and help close the racial wealth gap. As part of our effort, I convened a discussion about the future of higher education in California, featuring student debt strikers, organizers, and academics in early 2020. Hosted in collaboration with the Onassis Los Angeles, a center for dialogue, the encounter was designed to reflect more deeply on the Debt Collective's demands and tactics. What does "free public college" really mean? How could we best advance our agenda?

I began by inviting student debtors to tell their stories. Pamela Hunt, a student debt striker and single mother who went to a for-profit college, took the floor first. "I made my situation worse off going to college," she said. "The reason I did it was to take care of my family, and then it ended up where I really wasn't able to take care of them the way that I wanted to after all." Nathan Hornes, another Debt Collective member, recounted being told to play Monopoly for a class midterm in a similar program. Neither Hunt nor Hornes, who are both Black and working class, felt they could afford the luxury of studying for studying's sake—a pragmatism for-profits take advantage of, charging sky-high tuition for subprime vocational programs. Sociologist Tressie McMillan Cottom estimates that in 2008 there were more low-income Black and Hispanic women enrolled in for-profit institutions than in four-year public and private nonprofit colleges combined. A decade later, as the economy cratered once again, for-profits, with their false promises of economic advancement and online course offerings, were anticipating another enrollment surge.

That afternoon, the racial- and class-bound dimensions of student debt were immediately apparent. Millions of white people are also drowning in student debt—I know because I was once one of them—but our Black counterparts are weighted down more heavily. "It's really important, especially when we talk about building a movement, that we talk about commonality and common ground and that white working-class folks are dealing with some of the same challenges that people of color are," the historian Barbara Ransby observed during the conversation. "But racism and white supremacy do add another layer to it all. It's structural abandonment of communities. It's the precarity of life. It's racial profiling. Just getting on and off of predominantly white campuses is a navigation art."

Statistics bear witness to this imbalance. Before Covid wrecked the economy, the median wealth of white families was nearly eleven times more than the median wealth of Black families; the typical Black household headed by someone with an advanced degree possessed less wealth than a white household headed by someone with a high school diploma. The lack of family wealth makes borrowing more necessary, while workplace discrimination and wage disparities (and the fact that Black borrowers are more likely to be supporting older relatives) make repayment more challenging. A 2016 study found that Black people graduate with about $7,400 more in student debt than their white counterparts; four years after finishing school, that gap increased to $25,000. A 2019 study reported that twenty years after starting college, the typical white student owes 6 percent of their cumulative debt, or around $1,000, while the typical Black borrower still owes 95 percent, or around $18,500. As fees and interest accrue over years and decades, Black borrowers, and Black women in particular, end up paying significantly more for the same degrees than white borrowers do.

And they get less in return. At around eighty of the country's top colleges, more students are now admitted from the top 1 percent of the income ladder than the bottom 40 percent; more than two-thirds of students at the most selective colleges come from the country's top income quintile, while only 4 percent come from the bottom one. The richest students go to the richest schools, which inevitably spend the most money per student, advantage begetting advantage. Administrators are incentivized to attract wealthier recruits—"poorer students have lower average test scores and post-graduation incomes, which bring down schools' rankings in *US News and World Report*," as one article in the *New York Review of Books* explained—with the pandemic guaranteed to make their pursuit more frantic. In a desperate bid to win over well-to-do students, colleges are now offering more "merit"-based financial aid to those that need it least. "Rather than education leading to wealth, it is wealth that facilitates the acquisition of an expensive education," economists Darrick Hamilton and Trevon Logan have written. That investment then pays dividends over a lifetime.

Advertised as the great equalizer, college today has increasingly polarizing effects. While coddled upper-class children enroll at elite institutions on their parents' dime—and in, critical ways, on the public's, since private colleges receive an array of state subsidies, including tax breaks—the majority of students struggle mightily to have a chance to learn. Forty-five percent of students who enroll don't manage to graduate in six years, but the debt lingers on even if they don't get a diploma. It's not easy to finish a two- or four-year degree while homeless or housing insecure, as around 40 percent of students were in early 2020—and that was before Covid-related evictions and foreclosures swept the country.

As educational access has increased across the population, so too has economic inequality. The current system reflects and reinforces deeply entrenched disparities, strengthening the position of the already privileged. While colorblind in theory, in practice the US system of higher education is a costly and convoluted system of affirmative action for affluent white people.

* * *

We will not be able to remedy the crisis of higher education without coming to grips with the role racism has played in fueling it. In 2020, the average cost of attending a four-year private college was more than $200,000, an astonishing sum given that, a few generations earlier, college was often no or very low cost—back then, even the fees at some private institutions could be covered working a part-time minimum-wage job. But it was mainly white men who benefited from this arrangement. "When the UC system was a lot whiter, it was basically free," Dylan Rodríguez, who teaches ethnic studies at UC Riverside, said during the Onassis House discussion. As the student body became "Blacker, browner, more working class," a racist backlash pushed the state to defund education at all levels, forcing the most socioeconomically vulnerable people to pay out of pocket to attend ostensibly public institutions.

The person most responsible for this shift was Ronald Reagan, though it took decades for his revanchist policies to fully take root. When people tell the story of student debt and skyrocketing tuition, they typically begin in Berkeley, where students rose up against McCarthyism and the Vietnam War. Reagan propelled himself to the governor's mansion by attacking the protesters and vowing to "clean up that mess" on campus. In 1966, the newly elected governor proposed that, for the first time, the UC system charge tuition. Doing so would "get rid of undesirables," he said. "Those there to agitate and not to study might think twice before they pay tuition—they might think twice how much they want to pay to carry a picket sign." The state, he announced in a speech the following year, should not be "subsidizing intellectual curiosity."

As the sociologist Melinda Cooper argues in her insightful book *Family Values*, free public education—along with rising rages—meant that a generation of students were able to go to college without relying on their parents. Cooper sees the imposition of tuition and student debt as part of a concerted attempt to undermine this freedom and to reinstate what she calls "family responsibility." Privatization, in Cooper's account, has a double meaning: it means both state disinvestment in favor of market-friendly policies and a shift of responsibility from the public to the private sphere. To burden families alone with their children's fate is to put those families that lack inherited wealth because of centuries of racial oppression at an overwhelming disadvantage; it was also intended as a means to shore up waning patriarchal authority. Reactionary figures promoted student debt as a means to suppress social movements and discipline individuals. In their 1970 book *Academia in Anarchy*, neoliberal economists James M. Buchanan and Nicos E. Devletoglou argued that students should have to pay for their education so they would cease treating college as "psychedelic game." Samuel Huntington warned in 1975 that the democratization of higher education was fueling a "general challenge to existing systems of authority, public and private."

Racial anxiety was, of course, also in play, even when it was not explicitly stated. "People no longer felt the same compulsion to obey those whom they had previously considered superior to themselves in age, rank, status, expertise, character, or talents," Huntington lamented; attuned readers could hear the dog whistle. As historian Donna Murch demonstrates in her book *Living for the City*, the composition, and complexion, of California's student body was swiftly changing during Reagan's ascension. Until 1966, fewer than one hundred Black students out of a student body of twenty thousand are estimated to have attended Berkeley, but Black youth at the time were seeking educational opportunities in droves, flocking especially to junior colleges with the same determination that drove their parents to migrate from the South. By 1969, the San Francisco Bay Area and Los Angeles had the highest rate of Black college attendance in the country, with the Bay Area leading nationally in college completion. Hubs of study and debate, junior colleges became incubators of Bay Area Black radicalism.

In 1960, California's celebrated "Master Plan" committed to making postsecondary education available to every high school graduate at public expense; state policy makers saw higher education as crucial to Cold War economic development and national security. "In California in the fifties and sixties, people felt that they had a right to higher education," Murch told me. "The liberal state makes education free and by doing that, it actually produces a movement that fights the liberal state." Students took bold stances against racism, imperialism, and capitalism. Fifteen minutes away from Berkeley, Oakland's Merritt College nurtured the development of figures such as Bobby Seale and Huey Newton, who went on to found the Black Panther Party. They began their activist careers demanding Black studies curriculum and Black instructors. College, they argued, should reflect the community being served. Reagan, then, wasn't wrong to see a connection between free education and political dissent—he was wrong to want to suppress it.

Today, first-generation Black college students, like those who once gathered on the Merritt campus, are at risk of being targeted by predatory for-profit colleges, which spend hundreds of millions advertising to prospective students, rather than community colleges perpetually starved for funds. The right wing's attacks on higher education—and its promotion of rapacious, privatized alternatives—have to be understood as a conscious attempt to quell the kind of militant intellectualism that rocked the Bay Area in the late sixties. The attacks were also a way to achieve resegregation by other means—by denying state support and upward mobility to an increasingly nonwhite public. A combination of antiradicalism, racism, recessionary pressure, and right-wing anti-tax revolts emboldened Reagan's ravaging of the welfare state and simultaneous bolstering of the prison–industrial complex. Soon, California led the nation not in education but mass incarceration.

* * *

In 2020 the American Federation of Teachers surveyed adjunct university faculty and discovered an epidemic of poverty. Nearly a third of respondents reported earning less than $25,000 annually; nearly 25 percent said they rely on public assistance to survive, and 40 percent had trouble covering basic household expenses. One of many ironies of contemporary higher education is the fact millions of students are mortgaging their futures to pay for classes taught by people who may not make minimum wage. While administrator salaries bloated over the years, the percentage of part-time instructors barely scraping by exploded. Pre-Covid, almost 75 percent of college teachers were non-tenure-track. Of the more than half a million new professors hired to teach the millennial generation, 94 percent were "contingent." And then, due to Covid, instead of adding new jobs, schools downsized. City University of New York offered a taste of what was to come: by July 2020 it fired 2,800 people, most of them adjunct faculty.

Academia has long perpetuated, and profited from, the myth that no real work happens under its auspices—professors' mental labor is distinguished from menial drudgery, and graduate students are deemed apprentices not employees. Fortunately, there is a growing movement that rejects this obfuscation and demands the right to be unionized and properly compensated.

At the same time the Debt Collective was gathered in Los Angeles, graduate students across the University of California system were on a wildcat strike, defying their union and demanding a cost-of-living adjustment. They pointed out that their baseline stipends of just under $22,000 were paltry and barely provided enough to pay rent, compared to the nearly six hundred UC employees who took home over half a million dollars a year. When we spoke, Sucharita Kanjilal, a PhD candidate in anthropology, compared the situation for students who reside on campus to living in a "company town." Their meager remittances were all but eaten up by housing and insurance payments to the university.

Santa Cruz strikers, Kanjilal told me, weren't only fighting for better pay. They also called for "cops off campus," a demand that, though initially dismissed as quixotic, proved prescient when protests against police brutality swept the globe a few months later. In Santa Cruz, the university reportedly spent $300,000 a day for additional security, while a public records request revealed that it had also deployed military surveillance equipment to monitor the protests. Meeting the strikers' demand of an increase of $1,412 per student per month for all 1,800 graduate students would have cost $2.5 million a month—significantly less than paying the cops who beat and arrested strikers for a comparable period. The decision to increase spending on policing, not teaching, raises the perennial question of budget priorities. As Hannah Appel, a cofounder of the Debt Collective and a professor at UCLA, told me, "We have had these problems for a long time. Now the administration can conveniently be like, 'Oh, Covid, sorry, we're going to lay you off.'" If faculty don't fight back, administrators across the country will seize this disaster to further restructure universities in line with corporate management principles.

At Rutgers University in New Jersey, faculty and staff did just that. A public university system made up of seventy-one thousand students and thirty thousand workers across three campuses, Rutgers declared a "fiscal emergency" after spending $50 million to refund students for unused campus services in spring 2020 and seeing its state appropriations plummet. Before the emergency was declared, a coalition of unions representing twenty thousand workers offered a work-sharing proposal that would have saved Rutgers $100 million by using strategic furloughs to prevent any layoffs. Building off an organizing model known as Bargaining for the Common Good developed by K–12 educators, the guiding principle is to defend the most vulnerable—in this case, dining and part-time teaching staff.

In 2019, such a holistic framework helped AAUP-AFT, the faculty and graduate student union, secure higher wages, win pay equalization across the three campuses, implement measures to ensure gender and racial equity, and more—a contract Donna Murch, who teaches history at the New Brunswick campus, told me was "remarkable." "Part of our fight is to try to get tenured faculty to identify with people that make less money and have less job security," Murch explained, and to use their relative privilege to fight for more than their own bread-and-butter concerns.

Administrators dragged their feet and never responded to the work-sharing offer, undermining their claims that the cuts had been triggered only by budget concerns. They also were not transparent about the university's $600 million unrestricted reserve fund, which union organizers believed should be used to prevent layoffs. Nor did they demand a significant sacrifice from the university's football coach, who was in his first year of an eight-year $32 million contract (he agreed to a 10 percent pay cut for four months). Instead, administrators fired more than one thousand people—three hundred of them adjunct faculty whose dismissals saved $4 million—and continued to write checks to the notorious anti-union law firm Jackson Lewis, which charged the university $1.6 million between 2018 and 2020.

The struggle in New Jersey, as in countless other places, was not really about saving money so much as how to spend it. It was a struggle over power. "Rutgers has about three hundred people working in the top administration," Todd Wolfson, the president of the AAUP-AFT, told me. They are the ones who decide to hire adjuncts and pay them poorly; they are the ones who invested tens of millions of dollars in athletics, not academics; they are also the ones who made up the Covid-19 planning committee, relying on a unilateral process when what was really needed was union, student, and community representation to help guide the university through an unprecedented crisis. A democratically governed university is the last thing administrators want to see—but it is the only thing that can ensure the long-term survival and safety of the institution and those who depend on it.

"We see the thirty thousand people who are making a life serving this institution, serving the students, maintaining our buildings, serving us lunch, also teaching and doing research, as the people who should be making the decisions about the university," Wolfson said. He wants to see the creation of a Rutgers workers' council where people run the university collectively. "That doesn't mean every one of us makes every decision together," Wolfson clarified. "But together we need to lift our voices and help reorient the university because it's lost its way." Wolfson pointed to the absence of a student voice on the board of governors of the university as an example of the problems that stem from a lack of representation. "Not one student has any role in any decision-making, which is why you see tuition hikes." As Murch declared in a piece for the *Chronicle of Higher Education*, "All of us have a stake in this, and all of us should have a say."

* * *

Before the historic wave of protests for Black lives began in May of 2020, the semester was already overwhelming for twenty-one-year-old Jael Kerandi, a rising senior at the University of Minnesota. "There's no manual on how to be student body president during the pandemic," she told me. But when she got wind of George Floyd's murder a few miles from her campus, she knew exactly what she had to do. In an eloquent and indignant open letter, Kerandi confronted university administrators who claimed to have values of diversity, equity, and inclusion and yet hired police to patrol campus who had a record of murdering Black men and women. She demanded the school cut off its relationship to the Minneapolis Police Department and gave them twenty-four hours to respond. "Attending a predominantly white institution, most of my constituents are white," said Kerandi, who is Black. "But students have been asking for these things for years and those voices have gone unheard for so long." Before the deadline was up, the school committed to stop contracting with MPD for support during large campus events and specialized services.

Even though colleges as we know them were shut down due to Covid, incredible learning still took place. White Americans were far more supportive of the protests for racial justice than they had been of similar actions in the past. Millions joined marches, and civil disobedience became commonplace. People began reading about and discussing the nation's history, the dynamics of racial capitalism, and the possibility of not only prison reform but also prison abolition. A reckoning, unimaginable only a short while before, appeared to be under way.

As the educator Jason Wozniak pointed out to me, the Greek word *scholé* means free time, suspension, contemplation, and delay. School, in this sense, is not so much a place as a circumstance, one with a distinct time frame. It may be that the pandemic shifted people's collective sense of time in ways that allowed some to face and reflect on truths they might, under normal conditions, continue to avoid—truths about oppression, exploitation, vulnerability, and interdependence. The moment also calls to mind an insight from historian Robin D. G. Kelley: "Social movements generate new knowledge, new theories, new questions. The most radical ideas often grow out of a concrete intellectual engagement with the problems of aggrieved populations confronting systems of oppression." Learning has never been an activity confined to campus; it often happens in the streets and through struggle. Because of the pandemic, millions of people were able to pay serious and sustained attention to the causes and the stakes of these protests. The university as it is currently constructed validates and cultivates certain kinds of erudition and expertise while discounting other forms of knowledge and experience. The protests for Black lives, the attempts by Rutgers staff to change their working conditions, and the Debt Collective's student debt strike are all pedagogical experiments that open space for participants to be thinking, engaged democratic subjects.

Even when they were shut down, colleges were still implicated in the uprisings. On June 2, the Los Angeles Police Department turned UCLA's Jackie Robinson Stadium into a field jail where they detained protesters who were demonstrating past curfew. Hannah Appel is part of a coalition of faculty members who denounced the collaboration. "Universities have turned racial justice into a brand," she told me. But truly supporting racial justice means doing much more than naming buildings for civil rights icons and then arresting demonstrators in their shadows. A more profound transformation is required.

During the Debt Collective's dialogue, Barbara Ransby invoked the concept of abolition in the context of education, noting that abolition is a framework that conjures not merely the dismantling of oppressive systems but also the creation of new social arrangements of solidarity and care. "We know a lot of bad things and bad structures exist," Ransby said. "We're not as rehearsed in what to replace them with." Simply canceling student debt and eliminating tuition is not enough to yield educational equity in a society serrated by inequality. Instead, we need schools that are not only free in cost but also aimed at widening the sphere of democratic freedom. Appel articulated this clearly when we spoke: "Just because you don't pay for it doesn't mean it's free of white supremacy. It doesn't mean it's free of repressive cops or that it is a sanctuary from state violence." Tuition-free school isn't enough if only elites can successfully compete for limited spots, or if schools that serve poor and working students remain immiserated and understaffed. That is why Christopher Newfield, one of the foremost chroniclers of the political economy of higher education, argues that advocates must set their sights not just on free public college but also on more equitable funding structures. He suggests $20,000 per student per year as a spending floor to guarantee that disadvantaged students have a fair shot at academic success.

If the Covid crisis has revealed anything, it is that we have the money. It is possible to reverse decades of privatization. The pandemic has also revealed that the only democratic and sustainable revenue source for higher education is public funds. (A debate about whether private colleges should exist—they don't in many countries—is long overdue.) Universities may be subject to austerity at the state level, but the federal government made trillions of dollars appear out of thin air as part of its coronavirus relief packages. "There is scarcity," economist Stephanie Kelton, who worked on the original College for All legislation, explained at the Debt Collective's gathering in Los Angeles. "We can run out of trained professors, we can run out of classrooms, we can run out of parking spaces." But this scarcity is material, not monetary. "The one thing that the federal government can't run out of is its own currency. . . . Elected officials have enormous power to take out their pens and their pads and to sit down and to look at that budget line by line and decide where to invest." A budget,

Kelton often says, is a moral document, a reflection of social priorities. The financing is the easy part—mustering the political will and enough congressional votes to make it happen is hard. That will require a militant mass movement ready to challenge not only Republicans but also centrist Democrats who have perpetuated policy failures instead of addressing root problems.

This country has made bold moves before, and not only at the federal level. In 1930, in the throes of the Great Depression, Brooklyn College was founded. "The school was envisioned as a stepping stone for the sons and daughters of immigrants and working-class people toward a better life through a superb—and at the time, free—college education," the official website declares. In the 1960s, Black and Puerto Rican students across the City University of New York system faced police repression to push things farther, demanding open admissions so their working-class peers could have the same opportunities. They won their case, and the student body rapidly diversified. But as was the case in California, a combination of racist backlash and recession-driven austerity thwarted progress, undoing the activists' hard-won reforms.

Half a century later, the CUNY students' vision for higher education still resonates: they insisted that universities should be both free and open, that public institutions should reflect and serve their communities, and that students should play a role in university decision-making. They also critiqued the concept of meritocracy, insisting that vital knowledge is produced both inside and outside the ivory tower. The students who called for open admissions at CUNY understood that rejecting meritocracy did not mean rejecting rigor or discipline, but rather acknowledging that traditional conceptions of merit veil class and race inequities. They wanted to democratize access to academic excellence on the grounds that education is a right, not a privilege or a commodity. The state, they maintained, should subsidize curiosity. And yet even if we were to revolutionize higher education in line with their prescriptions and went even farther—shutting down for-profits, eliminating tuition, opening admissions, improving and equalizing access and quality across the board—many social problems would persist. More and better education alone will not solve our economic woes, and an abundance of college degrees will not make more and better-paying jobs magically appear. If that is our goal, we need a federal jobs guarantee and stronger unions, not more undergraduates. In any case, a college degree, even a free one, should not be a prerequisite to a fair wage and dignified life.

Covid-19 is a crisis of terrifying proportions. The struggle ahead is over how we respond to it. History shows this response will be shaped, to a large degree, by the persistence of structural racism on the one hand, and our commitment to racial justice on the other. We can seize this moment and remake the university into something that is inclusive and liberating or reinforce long-standing and destructive inequities. If we choose the former path, everyone will benefit. It is clear that millions of working- and middle-class white people also pay a steep price to maintain the racist, segregated status quo.

Public colleges and universities were free not that long ago. They can be free again. But as Hannah Appel told me, we need to define our terms. What does "public" mean? "The unqualified public has always been the white male public in this country," Appel said. That's why she argues that we must insist not just on universal public goods but also *reparative* ones. We need systems designed to both acknowledge our unequal past and actively repair and redress ongoing harms. Only if we do that can the university live up to its name, embodying the Latin *universitas*, which means "the whole" or "the world"—a space for everyone, where no subject is off-limits.

8

WHO, THE PEOPLE?

At the center of the idea of democracy lies an intellectual abstraction, an abstraction that renders democracy, almost by definition, a distinctly challenging form of government. Stripped to its basics, democracy means rule of the people (*demos*, people, and *kratia*, rule). This means figuring out just who the people who allegedly rule actually *are* always requires some baseline level of theoretical engagement. It's not as obvious as pointing to a picture of a monarch and saying, "That's the ruler." Over the centuries, all sorts of details—from the ornate headgear to the strange habit of marrying family members—symbolized a single individual's sovereignty over a population. In royal social orders, the king or the queen makes the decisions, and "the people" are irrelevant. No one administering the government cares what the peasants think. But who, or what, do you point to in a democracy to symbolize the status of the people as their own rulers? The very notion of a democratic people is an idea, and an elusive one at that, not a real tangible thing. "The people" isn't self-evident

* Previously published as "Who, the People? The Central Truths of Democracy Are Not Always Self-Evident," *Baffler*, no. 43 (January 2019).

or whole. It is constructed, contingent, and constantly shifting. "The people," in this sense, don't actually exist.

We could, I suppose, just be lazy and point to elected officials as the avatars of our will—they are literally our "representatives," after all. But doing so would not only be yielding to a formal technicality—it would also be a rather morale-deflating exercise, given all the disappointing specimens who find their way into office. What's more, it would also be inaccurate. During the wave of pro-democracy Occupy protests that kicked off in Spain and Greece before spreading to the United States in 2011, there was a chant that could often be heard shouted by masses of people outside government buildings: "You don't represent us!" Wherever this slogan rang out, people meant the same thing: the individuals in power don't stand for the people, or stand up for them—and given the money-driven and compromised condition of Western democracies long hailed as the vanguard of expansive popular representation, it's hard to argue the point.

* * *

How, then, might we instead go about envisioning the people? How can we represent them in a way that rises to the challenge and honors the complexity of the task at hand? The most suggestive, and instructive, way to tackle the riddle of popular sovereignty as a visual proposition might be to review some of the best-known efforts to render the people as self-conscious political subjects in Western art. To begin understanding how to see the people as they might one day be, we'd do well to get a better grasp of how they have been formerly, and formally, portrayed.

Consider, for example, the iconic *Liberty Leading the People*, composed in 1830 by Eugène Delacroix and held in the Louvre's permanent collection. Standing amid carnage, against a background of gray smoke, Lady Liberty holds a musket in one hand and the tricolor flag of the republic in another while wearing a red Phrygian cap, that unmistakable Jacobin symbol. A brave child waves a pistol at her side, while a young man stands holding a hunting shotgun to her right, a top hat perched on his head, symbolizing the poor and the petty bourgeois in revolt together. The rebellious crowd also includes a figure of a craftsman or worker and a student. Here is an image of the people in the throes of their own revolutionary assurance—beleaguered and injured, yes, but fully aware that they're being summoned forward, and into power, by the ineluctable logic of history. They are justified in their armed insurrection.

For a more recent gloss on the people's destiny, we could turn to Diego Rivera's Depression-era *Detroit Industry Murals*, a series in homage to Ford Motor Company's industrial might and innovation. Rivera spent months observing Ford's River Rouge plant and sketching drafts. His finished work portrays burly men building mechanical wonders, together with a powerful suggestion of the hazards and horrors entailed in such work—automobile assembly lines juxtaposed with the manufacture of poison gas. In the 1950s, after Rivera's Marxism triggered McCarthyite opposition, museum officials posted a disclaimer:

> Rivera's politics and his publicity seeking are detestable. But let's get the record straight on what he did here. He came from Mexico to Detroit, thought our mass production industries and our technology wonderful and very exciting,

painted them as one of the great achievements of the twentieth century. . . . If we are proud of this city's achievements, we should be proud of these paintings and not lose our heads over what Rivera is doing in Mexico today.

In 2013, in the wake of another economic crisis, the once proud city declared bankruptcy and almost had to sell Rivera's murals to assuage its creditors. The Ford Foundation, with other philanthropic groups, swooped in to save the day. In contrast to Delacroix's effort to conjure the people as the confident augurs of a new democratic age, this is an image of the people both empowered and stymied on the path to realizing a fuller, substantively democratic livelihood. They are both the creators and casualties of the Industrial Age.

* * *

In a similar vein, one of the best-known, and most candid, New Deal murals is made up of twenty-seven panels, gracing what was then San Francisco's main post office. Instead of creating a triumphalist image of a benevolent, heroic working people typical of the period, artist Anton Refregier painted California's history riven by prejudice and oppression. One panel shows the violent divisions of the Civil War playing out in San Francisco's Union Square; another honors a 1934 dock workers strike during which two longshoremen were killed and many others injured; another unflinchingly portrays Irish workers viciously beating Chinese immigrants accused of stealing jobs. Beneath this panel is an 1875 quote from Irish labor leader Frank Roney: "Attacks upon the Chinese I consider unreasonable and antagonistic to the principles of American Liberty."

When they were unveiled at the height of the New Deal's campaign to present a "popular front" of support among home-grown Americans for the burgeoning welfare state, the murals were hugely controversial: What kind of propaganda *was* this? critics demanded. (Criticism came from all corners. According to one account, "The Catholic Church protested that a friar preaching to Indians at Mission Dolores was too fat; Refregier slimmed him.") The complaints stemmed, in part, from the public's own material stake in Refregier's project: it's no coincidence that his installation marked one of the final public paintings of their kind supported by the federal government. In a fit of Cold War paranoia, then-Congressman Richard Nixon tried to have them destroyed. Refregier insisted on presenting the past not as a romantic backdrop for a pat celebration of the status quo but as a prelude to contemporary strife that must be reckoned with. This tense and unresolved depiction of America's mythic mass democracy is perhaps most familiar to those of us who, with mounting alarm, have tried to chronicle the battered democratic polis of our current populist and polarized era—a vision of the people beset by ethnic, racial, and class conflict.

And of course there's Norman Rockwell and his famous renderings of Franklin Roosevelt's *Four Freedoms*: *Freedom of Speech*, *Freedom of Worship*, *Freedom from Want*, and *Freedom from Fear*. Rockwell's sequence of portraits, commissioned to help sell war bonds, are still some of the most widely circulated images in US history. They show a middle-aged white man letting his opinion be known at a New England town meeting; white heads bowed in worship at church; a happy white family sitting down to a holiday feast; white parents tucking in their white children to sleep. This might be termed the people's mass apotheosis—an image of contented, consuming people who are still called upon to protect their way of life (only not, significantly, at the squalid and blood-soaked barricades of Paris but through strategic purchases and investments in self-defense and future stability).

Or, finally, we could gaze at *The Verdict of the People*. This canvas was painted by Missourian George Caleb Bingham in 1855—and was granted pride of place by Donald Trump's handlers for a photo-op of the newly sworn-in president at his postinaugural luncheon. The press release from Senator Roy Blunt, who requested the painting, highlighted the seeming diversity of the crowd: "Bingham's electorate is one of inclusiveness," he insisted. But historians quickly clarified that the image actually depicts the electoral victory of a proslavery candidate in a small-town antebellum race. The artist thus offers a less-than-flattering verdict of his own: witness the people as an elective body who have chosen something awful and are pleased as punch about it.

Looking back on these variegated renderings of the people with the chastened benefit of hindsight, it's immediately apparent that many are left out. The paradoxical effect of this whitewashed and patriarchal iconography is that it also forcefully highlights the presence of people who aren't white or male whenever they happen to appear. Delacroix's painting, of course, dates from a time when women weren't fully enfranchised citizens, but Lady Liberty's exposed and heaving bosom occupies the front and center of the canvas. And in *The Verdict of the People*, a single Black man is featured prominently, selling moonshine at the bottom left of the frame—perhaps Bingham's suggestion that despite all the controversy over slavery, African Americans were not to be regarded as suitably virtuous and self-disciplined democratic subjects. Being unseen or overexposed produces the same cruel effect—marking populations as insignificant and excluded.

This stable of imagery again brings us back to the central quandary of democratic theory: Who counts as the people, and how can that definition be substantively revised and updated in view of shifting historical circumstances? Or to rephrase things in the language of iconography: Who is visible? Who is forced into the shadows? Self-government is a perpetual battle over who is in and who is left out, and we are living at a moment when this abiding struggle appears to be reaching a crescendo. At the same time, though, these questions, and the challenges they pose to representation, always lurk below the surface, even in periods of relative political calm.

* * *

Today this struggle is increasingly understood as a symptom of a populist resurgence, not as a challenge intrinsic to democracy. According to the conventional wisdom, populism defines "the people" against a corrupt elite, and today elites are being spurned the world over. A growing class of liberal pundits tarnish every political stance they don't approve of as "populist," as though any mention of "the people" is an aberration from the liberal democratic status quo. (It's only by this deeply ahistorical and analytically bankrupt insistence that supposedly erudite commentators could compare "populist" Donald Trump to "populist" Bernie Sanders, despite the former leader's xenophobia and racist pronouncements and policies, and the latter's overt, inclusive pluralism.) By the distorted logic of our new cohort of antipopulist liberal thinkers, those who denounce Wall Street kleptocrats and self-serving

CEOs as enemies of working people are but the mirror image of right-wingers fulminating against immigrants, feminists, queers, and an all-powerful "politically correct" establishment. All one has to do, it seems, to claim a high-profile media sinecure or political science professorship, is to simply incant the bogey-word *populism*, and poof—like magic—the left and democratic socialism disappear, together with the specter of longer-term economic displacement and discontent that lie at the actual core of the revolt against neoliberalism in our time.

The reactionaries who cynically exploit this global mood of revolt from below are genuinely influential and more than a little terrifying. But there's nothing to be gained, analytically, by casually caricaturing their rise, their rhetoric, and their ideological worldview as "populist." Worse, for committed democrats who have long struggled to make the promise of self-rule a substantive aspect of our productive lives, there is much to lose. A whole spectrum of political possibility is being wantonly sacrificed—specifically the unique democratic heritage of the People's Party, dating from the turn of the twentieth century.

* * *

In place of the firm insistence by Gilded Age capital-*P* Populists and neo–Gilded Age democratic socialists that democracy should redress the market predations of industrial-age plutocrats, right-wing faux populists have abetted the continued upward consolidation of wealth and the steepening social chasms of inequality. Trump and his opportunistic immitators have focused exclusively on putative cultural affronts to the white forgotten man, who is incongruously figured as both unjustly marginalized and reassuringly universal. This debased political theology promotes the farce that "the people" is a stable entity, a pale-skinned self-evident ruling caste bound by blood, soil, Make America Great Again hats, and tiki torches. In order for them to be restored to their rightful place at the head of cultural and political life, the faithless institutions and political forces that have orchestrated their betrayal need to be cleansed—immigrants expunged and fenced out, college campuses clamped down on, patriarchs reaffirmed, and so forth. And the same logic holds for the allied reactionary movements lately seizing power in Europe. The over-the-top rhetoric of ethno-nationalist Nigel Farage reveals just how absurd such a framework is. When celebrating the outcome of the Brexit referendum, he crowed that the vote was a "victory for real people," thereby making the 48 percent of the British electorate who cast their ballots for the UK to stay in the European Union somehow unreal.

Such pronouncements are both transparently vile and inane—and bound to sow greater disaffection among the very working-class constituencies whose material grievances they crudely distort and exploit. But they do represent another backward-tending redoubt in the longer-term battle over who counts as the people and who doesn't—not, as some want to believe, a shocking anomaly or foreign intrusion that can be disavowed as "not who we are" (whoever that "we" may be). As we've seen, this tension is central to democracy itself, but it is *especially* central to US democracy, which was born of a constitutional compromise that counted Black human beings as fractions of a person.

Against this backdrop, we must experiment with ways of symbolizing the demos that do not mark some people as categorically "unreal" or otherwise less than others. Even more urgently, we need to marshal into the center of public life the self-representation of groups who have been erased, stereotyped, and otherwise diminished in conventional portrayals of the people. As Lawrence Goodwyn, the author of the definitive 1976 history of the American Populist movement, said about the actual legacy of Populism for would-be reformers of modern corporate capitalism, "The people need to 'see themselves' experimenting in democratic forms."

The challenge, then, is how to do all of this in a way that's not hackneyed, propagandistic, or sentimental. Contemporary advertisements pay saccharine tribute to the notion of diversity because corporations are seeking consumers, not citizens, and they'll take anyone's money in their quest to amass profits. How do we portray the people as a unity without papering over the shocking inequalities that define the status quo?

This question is far from an abstraction for me. I spent three years making a documentary called *What Is Democracy?*, and as I wrestled with that question I was also forced to grapple with the people who are definitionally bound to redefine democracy in its next phase of development. I'm sure there are plenty of ways in which I fell short, but I didn't take the challenge lightly. I tried to make it clear that the film was by no means a definitive portrait, including a polyphony of voices while not subsuming the uniqueness of individuals. I tried to emphasize not just diversity but solidarity, not just inclusion but transformation. I tried to show a democratic people not limited by a single nation or strict conception of citizenship. I also tried to show the demos in action, not in the quiescent repose of Norman Rockwell's reveries, but in the daily struggle to have one's needs and desires included on the agenda of a political order that has grown militantly hostile to anything resembling social democracy. Most of all, I tried to show how the stubborn question of who counts as the people continues to be contested and challenged on multiple levels, and that some people are quite literally fighting for their lives in its shadow. This meant, in other words, that I was charged with showing both the promise of democracy and its all-too-plain disappointments. The people aren't always pretty. I also tried to show, as Rivera and Refregier had, that this ugliness can translate directly into hateful bigotry and material exploitation.

* * *

Making my documentary often felt like a quixotic undertaking. It was, for starters, an effort to translate a central problem of political philosophy to the screen—which is not, to put things mildly, a recipe for runaway success at the box office. Beyond such formal constraints, I also found myself struggling with the same visual quandary that the fistful of artworks I've mentioned here sought to resolve: I had to at least attempt to represent the demos in a way I felt was fair and generous. But can't a more accurate, if exhausting and demoralizing, portrait simply be gleaned by visiting the bowels of an internet message board or reading user-generated comments? Does scrolling through an algorithmically generated social media feed offer a window straight into the soul of the people, in all our fragmentation, distraction, and impotent rage?

Though a feature film might seem a bit antiquated in an age of snapchats and dark posts, at least I wasn't working with oil and pigment. As Alexander Provan notes in an excellent 2017 essay in *Art in America*, the traditional painters who set out to represent the people to the best of their creative ability have long been replaced by "a panoply of professionals" who claim to uncover the preferences of the people through new methods of data harvesting. "The imagination of the artist," Provan writes, "has been surpassed by the techniques of the behavioral economist, filmmaker, advertiser, pollster, lobbyist, data scientist, and social media analyst. And politicians have become mediums through which messages are tested and refined, demographics are established and tweaked." Today's politicians run data-driven campaigns, creating proposals based on data sets from focus groups, reaching and mobilizing their constituents using precision targeting. In this age of rampant digital personalization, who needs "the people" anymore?

Our fast-fragmenting and notoriously insular mediasphere appears to make the project of coherently depicting the people all the more hopeless. But perhaps in every crisis of representation lies opportunity—if you are employed in the field of data collection and analytics, at least. The visual challenges of imagining and conjuring the people has been superseded by the pseudoscience of measuring and marketing their demographic self-images to them—to us. But "the people"—whatever the people is—is not just the aggregated preferences of millions of atomized individuals, a lowest-common-denominator pabulum of averages, as pollsters would have us believe.

Paintings may have been replaced by polling, but the results are not necessarily more accurate, and arguably even less so. Isn't that the distressing moral of how the presidential balloting played out in 2016? Liberal-leaning media experts and political professionals mistook the high-tech vision of the demos that they themselves had assiduously polled and marketed to as the actually existing electorate right up until election night, with the disastrous results we are now living through. They forgot their models and predictions were representations, believing them instead to be the real thing. The gap between image and actuality was profound. The *New York Times* forecast gave Clinton "an 85 percent chance to win" while the experts at the Princeton Election Consortium put the probability (at one point just days before the election) as "greater than 99 percent," and Clinton's campaign, using its own polling, came to similar self-affirming conclusions. Pew Research later claimed the discrepancy was due to something called nonresponse bias: "It is possible that the frustration and anti-institutional feelings that drove the Trump campaign may also have aligned with an unwillingness to respond to polls." Liberals eagerly took what was, in fact, angry silence to be a sign of nonexistence. The best methods money could buy couldn't detect millions of people who weren't on board the Democratic train.

* * *

Republicans, meanwhile, aren't so easily deceived, and only because they are more cynical. Conservatives don't care about the people and have always been content to rule as a minority. They want to rule as a fragment of the people—a very rich and powerful fragment. But occasionally even they need a fig leaf. Remember "Joe the Plumber" Wurzelbacher from the 2008 campaign trail? Here was the voice of the people challenging Obama's nefarious plan to "spread the wealth" at the steep expense of heroically aspiring business owners like himself—even though his name was not Joe, but Samuel, and he wasn't the entrepreneurial licensed plumber he claimed to be, but an uncertified plumber's assistant. Wurzelbacher was promptly hailed as a hero of the misunderstood working class and elevated as a worthy, if ultimately unsuccessful, candidate for Congress himself.

Trump himself likewise made enthusiastic use of such prop figures of demotic authenticity, such as Diamond and Silk—the two Black sisters and erstwhile Democrats whose videos, where they animatedly affirm the president's every word, attract hundreds of thousands of views. Watching their shenanigans online, it can be tempting to dismiss them as unreal, given their over-the-top adulation for Trump, unhinged rants, and opportunistic arguments (upset at declining Facebook traffic, Diamond invoked the specter of segregation, decrying a "new Jim Crow . . . to suppress the voices of conservatives"). But I can report they are, in fact, all too real: in 2016, as I was shooting *What Is Democracy?*, I ran into the duo on the highway as they were en route to a Trump campaign stop in Raleigh, North Carolina. And sure enough, a couple of hours later I saw them onstage, cheered on by an enthusiastic throng. "This election will decide whether we are ruled by a corrupt political class . . . or whether we are ruled by the people," Trump announced to the crowd later in the hour. "We're going to be ruled by the people, folks." With the aid of a pair of Black figureheads made prominent by virtue of the conspicuous absence of people like them within the broader Trump insurgency, the sorry spectacle updated the long-standing quandary of popular representation for an age of recursively fragmenting participation in civic life. It's now up to us to envision and project a different stable of images—based on a new set of viable political coalitions—to revive the old Populist quest to lend experimental and material dimensions to the democratic forms currently banished to the margins of the picture. We, the unreal people, must find ways to make ourselves seen and heard.

9

OUR FRIENDS WHO LIVE ACROSS THE SEA

A bronze, life-size male figure carrying a suitcase mounts a massive set of stairs to a jetliner that does not exist. He is slightly hunched, frozen midstep. Whatever the statue was initially intended to signify, it became a metaphor for the six thousand people stranded at Ellinikon, a derelict airport thirty minutes from the center of Athens, Greece. The sculpture stands in front of a wire fence, behind which most of the refugees live. Faded boarding passes litter the ground, as though all the airport customers suddenly dematerialized, only to be replaced by a new generation of travelers. Thanks to the closure of the Macedonian border in March of 2016 and a controversial deal between the European Union and Turkey, announced soon after, a new generation was stopped in its tracks, immobilized like the man cast in metal.

Before visiting Greece that spring, I had never given much thought to what limbo feels like, but now I know it is crushing. Greece's fifty thousand refugees and migrants are part of

---

* Previously published as "Our Friends Who Live across the Sea," *Baffler*, no. 31 (June 2016).

a larger wave of more than one million people who arrived in Europe in 2015. They came primarily from Syria, Afghanistan, and Iraq, but also Pakistan, Iran, Kurdish territories, Somalia, Sudan, Eritrea, and elsewhere—men and women, old and young, parents and their offspring, and thousands upon thousands of children traveling unaccompanied by adults. While EU member countries squabble about how to stop the influx, the de facto strategy has been one described by investigative journalist Apostolis Fotiadis as "militarization and externalization." Huge chunks of budgets that could have been allotted to humanitarian purposes were redirected to border security, biometrics, and surveillance; NATO warships returned migrants to Turkey, as Frontex, the EU's border agency, patrolled the coastlines; curtailed rescue missions meant thousands were left to drown in the Aegean and Mediterranean Seas, two favored migratory routes. Fear of terrorism was invoked not just to keep people fleeing terror away but also to justify killing them through a strategy of neglect.

"Do not ask me about the boat ride," Abid told me, shuddering. Abid was twenty-one and had made his way to Ellinikon from Pakistan, where his family sought refuge from Afghanistan after his father was killed by the Taliban. After weeks of intense debate with his mother, whom he obviously loves dearly, he spent his savings on the dangerous voyage to Europe. He understood that there was now a good chance he'd be sent back to Turkey, and he radiated sadness bordering on despair.

The West speaks the language of universal rights while practicing exclusion, vetting individual asylum seekers as though refugee status is a privilege to be bestowed on a select few and not a legal entitlement for all human beings in need of protection. Policy makers, pundits, and angry internet commentators are determined to distinguish between those fleeing war and those seeking a better life, but the division between those who have "legitimate" asylum claims and those who can be categorized as "economic migrants" is as artificial as the borders that block people's movements. Poverty can be as deadly as combat, though the job of bureaucrats is to deny such complexities. In the words of Princeton professor Didier Fassin, refugees have been reconfigured from "victims of persecution entitled to international protection to undesirable persons suspected of taking advantage of a liberal system." This shift did not happen spontaneously. After World War II, workers were needed to help rebuild European nations that would soon be players in the Cold War, which meant various populations were welcomed into Western Europe first for their labor power and later for their symbolic pro-democracy, anticommunist significance. But today, unemployment is rising and Islamophobia has superseded the Red Scare.

Against this backdrop, Afghans like Abid were increasingly treated as job-hunting opportunists, though their country had been rocked by decades of conflict. Many more would be denied asylum and deported, as some already had been. The official bureaucratic rationale was coldly mathematical: unlike Syrians, for example, Afghans who reached Greece could not apply for "relocation" to a second EU country because in the past their asylum applications had fallen just below the threshold acceptance rate of 75 percent. The true ethnic, economic, and political calculus is, of course, even more complex and fatalistic. Afghans tend to be more impoverished than their comparatively affluent Syrian counterparts (many of the nearly five million Syrians who fled between 2011 and

2016 were once middle class—doctors, teachers, shopkeepers, with houses and cars), which makes them less desirable "human capital" for an increasingly neoliberal Europe. And the United States and the EU insist Afghanistan is safe, or at least safe enough to send people back to—the world's superpowers still don't want to admit that Operation Enduring Freedom was a blunder. If the war was a success, there cannot be legitimate refugees. I cannot fathom making an accusation of illegitimacy to Abid.

In impeccable English with an eloquence that is uniquely his, Abid told me he used to work as a language teacher. Now he was leading informal classes at the camp. What was an intelligent and ambitious young person in his position supposed to do? His former life was untenable, but his lot had not improved. When Abid spoke of the feeling of being "alone" and "abandoned" at Ellinikon, he suddenly appeared a million miles away from my side. I could have a conversation with him, and write about him later, but I could not pull him from out of the void and into my world of stability and comfort and access.

As our conversation unfolded, Abid sighed. His problems stemmed from the simple misfortune, he reflected in concise summation, "of being born in a poor country."

* * *

If Abid had arrived in Greece a month earlier, his story would be radically different. He would have been doggedly pushing north on the difficult journey through the Balkans—hoping to reach Germany, the place nearly everyone I spoke to held up as a kind of promised land.

Germany became the dream destination of the desperate after chancellor Angela Merkel was publicly shamed during a PR stunt gone awry. Breaking the script, a young, crying Palestinian girl asked why it was that her family might be deported in the coming months. Soon, Merkel made a dash for the high road and declared Germany a haven. In 2015, migrating individuals and families began hiring smugglers, boarding flimsy small boats and crossing the Aegean to reach Greek islands in unprecedented numbers: Greece was a pit stop on the path to Munich or Berlin. Following the EU's deal with Turkey, Greece became a holding pen. Germany, some expert observers said, wanted to stem the human tide without having to endure the negative publicity that would be associated with closing its borders; thus, the 2016 EU plan was designed to force Greece and Turkey to do that dirty work. For all the criticism the deal attracted—Amnesty International called it "a historic blow to human rights" and a "flagrant violation of EU and international law" that abused the global Refugee Convention; Doctors without Borders ceased work in the Moria detention center on the island of Lesbos, refusing to be "instrumentalized for a mass expulsion operation [with] no regard for the humanitarian or protection needs of asylum seekers and migrants"; the Council of Europe reported that "new arrivals are systematically detained in inadequate conditions on an uncertain legal basis"—it had the desired effect. The torrent of boats slowed to a trickle, but not because the problem had been solved.

"The only reason the refugee crisis is now in the spotlight lies in a banal but brutal fact: it has penetrated from the periphery of Europe to the heart of the European Union," Croatian theorist Srećko Horvat wrote. The unstated goal of the EU-Turkey deal was to reverse this trend. Thus, informal camps were being supplanted or replaced by prisonlike detention centers. Migrants who arrived on Greek shores after the date the new rules went into effect were apprehended, held, and processed by a system aimed at returning them to Turkey. (For every "irregular" migrant from Syria who illegally crossed over the Aegean and was sent to Turkey, Europe took one Syrian from Turkey who had gone through the official channels, though the total number of relocated people could not exceed seventy-two thousand. In return for its troubles, Turkey would get more than $6 billion and various special privileges that would otherwise be denied to a human-rights-suppressing autocracy.) Quarantined in Turkey, a country that already hosted more refugees than any other on earth, and a place not exactly known for its press freedom, refugees would be that much harder for privileged Westerners to see. With the flow of dinghies stemmed, there would be fewer outrage-stirring images of dead toddlers washing up on beaches frequented by sun-loving tourists. Obliviousness could be restored.

* * *

Early in the morning the day after the EU-Turkey deal went into effect, I visited the Port of Piraeus. For months the passenger ships had been bringing three to six thousand people a day. I watched the early-morning arrival of what would be one of the final ferry-loads of refugees from the islands, only now there was a new twist—a massive and growing tent city, where more than five thousand people were then estimated to be living (that number would diminish as officials moved residents to government-run camps). As the boat disgorged its human cargo, tourists first and then refugees, I intercepted a twenty-six-year-old Kurdish woman who would have fit in at any hip Brooklyn café and a thirty-nine-year-old Afghan mother whose nine-year-old nephew eagerly and sweetly translated Persian into English until she broke into tears, telling us she had lost a son and that as a woman traveling without a man she felt very afraid. The boy faltered, and I also fumbled for words. What could I possibly say to console her?

At Piraeus, the glistening water contrasted surreally with the drab sea of tents, where families attempted some normality. Mothers sponge-bathed their kids with ice-cold water, laundry hung to dry, people passed the time by playing soccer. Tents were remarkably orderly, with blankets neatly folded, and shoes always carefully placed outside the door. But not everyone had a tent, as the parents who asked me for a "house" made clear. Inside the port buildings, where people slept neck to neck, the first thing occupants signaled to me was that the place stunk, as if there was some way I could fail to notice.

Everywhere there were children, making the most of terrible circumstances, as children tend to do. The adorable faces, playful smiles, and constant embraces could almost cause one to forget what they had endured. Later, Alex Sinclair, a twenty-three-year-old Canadian who came with his mother and sister to volunteer after seeing the crisis on the news, showed me drawings collected from the port coloring station. In one, done in the style of a child aged five or six, marker lines in the upper left corner traced planes dropping bombs. On the right side was a stick figure of a little girl holding a Syrian flag, her chest oozing blood.

This drawing illustrates why people would continue to leave Syria, even as Frontex and national police managed to block them from reaching Northern Europe. If you've seen before-and-after photos of Aleppo, you know you would try to leave too. Salam, a twenty-year-old who not long prior had had meaningful work as a music teacher, told me her mother was shot while the family was home having tea. "Fsssssssssst," she said, imitating the sound of the bullet that lodged in her abdomen.

When the motor of Salam's small boat died in the middle of the Aegean, her younger brother Jousef fixed it, likely saving everyone aboard. He was only eighteen and already a hero, but one no nation would formally recognize.

* * *

During my visit, I frequently heard that there were two crises unfolding in Greece—the refugee crisis and also an economic one. The word *crisis*, in both cases, functioned as a euphemism. In the first, it passed off a long-term and predictable political disaster rooted in the failed wars in Afghanistan and Iraq as a sudden and unexpected emergency, or (in some analyses) a repercussion of the Arab Spring. In the second, it hid the fact that Greece's economic problems began long before the ostensibly left-wing Syriza government capitulated to creditors in 2015. (Greek politicians cooked the books to join the EU monetary union; Goldman Sachs trapped the public in a toxic swap deal at the turn of the millennium; as early as 2005 the International Monetary Fund warned of the country's "potentially explosive debt dynamics.") More fundamentally, and as any good Marxist will tell you, crises are not aberrations but are intrinsic to capitalism—or, to put it in the more contemporary jargon of Silicon Valley techies, crises are a feature and not a bug.

Young people I met in Athens reminded me that they had lived their adult lives against the backdrop of crisis, an emergency that became normalized. Many were forced to migrate themselves, to head north to Germany or Denmark or the United Kingdom to work, creating conditions of identification with others who had been uprooted and dreamed of improving their lot.

The Port of Piraeus is public property, and a port worker and union organizer told me she was proud that the state had allowed the refugees to use the space. But beyond the location itself and some very basic and inadequate sanitation, the port authority doesn't offer much. The infrastructure was made for tourists passing through, not thousands of permanent residents. While the Red Cross, United Nations High Commissioner for Refugees, and other NGOs had small outposts, almost everything provided to the refugees came from regular citizens—tents, clothes, and much of the food and health care. People opened their apartments and homes, giving refugees the chance to bathe or rest for an afternoon, and occasionally to stay indefinitely.

Most Greeks I spoke to chalked this up to their culture's tradition of hospitality, but there were more explicit political motivations at work. Spontaneous offers of individual assistance were matched by collective initiatives, the so-called solidarity structures that blossomed in the wake of the 2011 Syntagma Square anti-austerity movement. Just inside the boundary of an upscale neighborhood called Kolonaki, a high school that had been closed for more than five years was reopened by a group of activists to house more than three hundred people, including approximately two hundred children. The place was dilapidated, but it was infinitely better than Piraeus or

Ellinikon or countless other way stations, including the infamous Idomeni camp, on the Macedonian border, where more than ten thousand people languished in muddy fields.

Greece has long been a hub of these kinds of self-organized or autonomous efforts, and is rightfully famous among the anarchist diaspora as a result. In the United States, anarchists are lucky to have a bookstore or a bike shop, but in Athens they have a whole neighborhood, which is known as Exarcheia. There you will find numerous squats that house (and feed) dozens of refugees, and meet people who participated in grassroots solidarity missions on the islands, pulling rubber boats to the shore and providing for and protecting new arrivals. One longtime resident of Exarcheia told me of assisting a woman as she gave birth the second her precarious boat hit the rocky shore of Lesbos. He and his comrades don't use the word *refugees*, he said, since *refugee* is a term that designates an official status that can be granted or denied by the state. Instead they call them "our friends who live across the sea."

* * *

Now that I have returned home, the sea has expanded into an ocean. And instead of friends I can see and reach, I keep in touch with some of the people I met at the camps via a postmodern attenuated form of friendship, Facebook. Abid puts on a brave front on his page, but when I posted an article about a leaked plan to deport eighty thousand Afghans from Europe—"the Afghan elite will be rewarded with university places in Europe, under a new EU strategy to use aid and trade as 'incentives' to secure deportation agreements for economic migrants from 'safe' areas of Afghanistan," the

Telegraph reported—his anguish was expressed through a series of emoticons: shocked and crying faces and praying hands.

When we spoke at Ellinikon, Abid had mused about whether he and others should protest, to highlight the horrible conditions at the camp or the need for safe passage and open borders. But would demonstrating alienate citizens of their host country, or would it spur bureaucrats in Brussels to react, or would their efforts simply be ignored? This is one of the many dilemmas endured by millions of exiled and stateless people. They have no formal say over the policies that may well determine whether they live or die; they have virtually no political leverage. In theory, at least, citizens of more powerful nations have a voice—yet it is one we are collectively failing to raise.

In Greece no one asked me why Americans are not doing more to pressure our government to help refugees. Americans, it seems, are not held to a particularly high ethical bar. It is a question, however, that we must ask ourselves: What can those lucky enough to be born in rich countries do for the cause of common humanity? Others, including Abid, have sacrificed enough.

Protesting would be a place to start. While we share news stories of ultranationalist parties gaining ground in Europe, in the United States the xenophobes and warmongers have already won—without a peep of resistance. Donald Trump's inflammatory rhetoric about closing the US borders obscured the fact that as of April 2016 fewer than 1,300 of the 10,000 Syrians US federal officials promised to resettle in that fiscal year had been admitted—while 2.7 million Syrians were in Turkey, Germany had taken more than 500,000 Syrian refugees, and more than 25,000 had been resettled in Canada with an additional 16,000 applications approved or in process. Meanwhile, the outgoing Obama administration—Hillary Clinton and other State Department officials in particular—poured fuel on the flames engulfing the Middle East. In the press, the surge of refugees was often compared to the one unleashed by the Second World War—a war that projects an aura of humanitarianism and heroism, even though the United States took only a tiny percentage of those seeking refuge from the Holocaust. Americans would be better off remembering Vietnam, the war we are always enjoined to forget. It was a disastrous and failed campaign that ruined an enormous number of lives for a pointless cause—kind of like the wars in Iraq and Afghanistan. But beginning in 1975, we ultimately took 800,000 refugees from that region, proving, at the very least, that such things can be done.

Ignoring history—out of a mix of malice and idiocy—our would-be leaders pander to the jingoistic and intolerant among us. All the while, those who are less bigoted remain trapped in a binge-purge cycle of outrage and indifference. While quick to express solidarity with the residents of Paris or Brussels in the wake of horrible attacks, we do not automatically identify with members of families displaced by war at Port of Piraeus, seekers of asylum huddled in Idomeni, or an abandoned young person like Abid at Ellinikon. The months ticked by and Abid remained in limbo, neither a citizen with rights nor officially a refugee in the eyes of the state. He is a friend who crossed the sea, yet he is still being left to drown.

Coda

Nearly a year after I met him at Ellinikon, Abid made it to Germany. He traveled mostly by foot over the Balkan route. Initially, things went well. He was assigned to live at a camp with other refugees in a small town, he began learning German and excelled, and he even got a job and appeared to be on the path to being granted permanent status. But there were bigger machinations happening on the international stage. As public opinion shifted and far-right anti-immigrant parties began to surge, the German government cut a deal with Afghanistan, and soon deportations commenced. Abid's request for asylum was denied. The official decision left out many basic facts of his case, so I helped him hire a lawyer to appeal. While his stay was extended, there was no certainty or stability in sight. By early 2020, Abid was exhausted, depressed, and done with limbo. Worn down and feeling unwelcome, he agreed to get on a flight to a dangerous country he did not consider home. The silver lining, he told me, was that he would eventually get to see his mother again.

10

THE RIGHT TO LISTEN

On a gray winter afternoon in 2019, I found myself seated around a massive table with about forty others on the ground floor of the historic Jane Addams Hull-House Museum in Chicago. A group of curators had invited me to participate in "Parts of Speech," an exhibit consisting of six lectures by six artists held at venues across the city. Instead of a typical talk, where I'd speak from a stage or behind a lectern, I'd proposed hosting a debtors' assembly—a forum where people could share stories of their financial hardship.

I'd never hosted such an assembly before. As the participants (not "audience members") trickled into the room, I reminded myself that the event was supposed to be about listening, not talking. Even so, I couldn't resist making some opening remarks. I told the group that my work as an organizer and documentary filmmaker had led me to understand listening as a deeply political act, and an underappreciated one. I suggested that our lack of attention to listening

---

* Previously published as "The Right to Listen: As Citizens of a Democracy, We Need to Hear One Another. Why Can't We?," *New Yorker*, January 27, 2020.

connected to the larger crisis of American democracy, in which the wealthy and powerful shape the discourse while many others go unheard. After I'd finished, Laura Hanna, the codirector of the Debt Collective, reeled off statistics demonstrating that we live with Gilded Age levels of inequality. Then she invited people to share their stories. In that ornate, wood-paneled room, an ominous silence descended. Looking from one quiet face to another, I panicked. What if no one talked?

The first person to speak confessed to owing $150,000 in student loans; many people in his life were unsympathetic to his plight, he said, because he had studied art and not "law or something." A young woman began to cry. "I'm a first-generation student, I come from a family of poverty," she said. "Sorry if I get emotional, but I'm here with my little one, and I'm thinking about her future. I'm $175,000 dollars in student-loan debt, and that's a huge number." When she finished, the room burst into applause.

The dam broke. A young man spoke of a mental-health crisis that had caused his debt to balloon; it included ambulance and hospital bills that took three years to pay off. A middle-aged woman described herself as "teetering at that edge of poverty" after she quit her job because of racist comments made by a colleague; her high debt load meant she couldn't help her college-age son. Another woman explained that her $125,000 in student loans were overwhelming not just her but also her mother, who had taken many of them out on her behalf; she described the pain of feeling judged a failure when you are trying the best you can. An older man told how, after arriving as a refugee from Liberia, he'd thought education would be a lifeline. He'd gotten a degree in chemistry and then attended nursing school, but now the money he owed was a trap from which he couldn't escape.

As the forum progressed, the mood in the room changed. Some people listened silently. Others, taking it all in, felt emboldened to reveal hardships they'd been reluctant to divulge elsewhere. A few got fired up: after hearing others' stories, the crying woman asked, "How can this be legal?" A mountain of debt and shame was becoming visible—an overwhelming burden that was also a common bond. I'd suggested a debtors' assembly because I wanted to create a space in which both sides of the communicative coin—speaking and listening—could be valued equally. Even so, I found myself surprised by listening's power. Though I work on issues of inequality, I was stunned by how much suffering the circle held.

"We have two ears and one mouth so we can listen twice as much as we speak," the Stoic philosopher Epictetus wrote, two thousand years ago. That's long been one of my favorite quotes. The truth, though, was that it had been a long time since I'd had an opportunity to listen, silently and at length, to what many other people had to say. Afterward, walking in the cold, I couldn't help but think of listening as something we're all entitled to—a right we're often denied and that the assembly had just reclaimed. Today, we are constantly reminded of the importance of free speech and the First Amendment. We exalt freedom in the expressive realm. Is there some corresponding principle of listening worth defending?

* * *

The idea that the right to listen to one another should be defended in a democracy seems strange. That's probably because we lack a shared vocabulary or framework for understanding listening as a political act. We pay lip service to the idea of listening: stage-managed "town-hall meetings," at which politicians and candidates respond to curated questions from a screened audience, are a familiar part of the political landscape. In 2017, Mark Zuckerberg embarked on a highly publicized national "listening tour," which yielded photographs of him riding a tractor with a farmer, going to church in a small town, helping out on an automobile assembly line, and so on. No one really imagined that Zuckerberg would listen to anything the people he visited had to say. We expect powerful people to be talkers, not listeners.

Philosophers, too, have thought mostly about speech—biased, perhaps understandably, toward dazzling utterances. When Aristotle declared man a "political animal," he argued that what distinguishes us from other creatures is our capacity for rational discourse. Modern philosophers have developed a framework of "deliberative democracy" in which oration and argument, declamation and debate, play out in an idealized public sphere. Careers have been made studying "speech-act theory," which examines how certain verbal expressions do things in the world: a judge declaring a defendant "guilty," for instance, or a couple "married." A corresponding "listening-act theory" doesn't yet exist.

But to listen is to act; of that, there's no doubt. It takes effort and doesn't happen by default. As anyone who has been in a heated argument—or who's simply tried to coexist with family members, colleagues, friends, and neighbors—well knows, it's often easier not to listen. We can tune out and let others' words wash over us, hearing only what we want to hear, or we can pantomime the act of listening, nodding along while waiting for our turn to speak. Even when we want to be rapt, our attentions wane. Deciding to listen to someone is a meaningful gesture. It accords them a special kind of recognition and respect.

In 2015, as I began making *What Is Democracy?*—a film about the challenges and possibilities of self-government—I immediately remembered that one of the hardest things about beginning to shoot a new documentary is remembering how to listen. I had to make a concerted effort to bite my tongue, so as not to babble over my subjects, ruining the footage (the way I had, to my eternal embarrassment, during my first film shoot). I found that listening well, so that I could respond genuinely and substantively, was exhausting work.

One of the things I heard, when I listened, was that many of the people I spoke with—immigrant factory workers, asylum seekers, former prisoners, schoolchildren—simply assumed that no one was interested in listening to them. At a community center in Miami, I asked a group of teenagers if they ever discussed democracy at school. "Yes, but it's about branches of government," a boy said. "They don't ask us, 'How do you feel about the school?'" As far as the kids could tell, their opinions didn't matter to their teachers or the administrators in charge, and they didn't feel there was much they could do about it.

"My voice isn't going to change anything," a girl told me with a shrug. I asked them whether they thought the adults in their lives had more of a say than they did. "I don't think people of higher power really want to hear a Black mom that's poor in a ghetto," the girl responded matter-of-factly.

Similarly, a boy warned, an adult standing up for himself at work would only get into trouble. It was better not to speak out and "just get it over with." Their certainty about going unheard was painful to hear.

* * *

It wasn't just other people's voices that preoccupied me. When I began filming *What Is Democracy?*, I cringed at my own voice, which sounds nothing like the voices of the men who generally occupy positions of cinematic authority. For better and worse, my documentary sensibility has been shaped by male directors, such as Errol Morris, Adam Curtis, and Werner Herzog, whom viewers can often hear off-screen, asking probing questions or providing erudite commentary. I had fully absorbed the sound of the male auteur and sage.

Early in the filmmaking process, I stumbled across "The Public Voice of Women," an essay by the classicist turned television presenter Mary Beard. From antiquity onward, Beard traces the ways women have been muted and mocked, compared to braying donkeys and worse. She quotes the lecturer Dio Chrysostom—"the Golden Mouth"—who, in the second century AD, asked his audience to imagine what he considered to be a nightmare scenario: "An entire community . . . struck by the following strange affliction: all the men suddenly got female voices, and no male—child or adult—could say anything in a manly way. Would not that seem terrible and harder to bear than any plague?"

Over the centuries, we've been taught to believe that deep voices are deep. Margaret Thatcher, famously, took lessons with a speech coach at the National Theatre to learn how to lower her pitch. Theresa May has admitted to modulating her delivery in the House of Commons, lest she sound a "shrill note." I realized that I had a version of the same impulse. Beard's essay turned a dial in my head; I began to hear myself and others in new ways. Rewatching Herzog's films, for example, I found myself imagining how their reception might shift if they were narrated by a California Valley girl instead of a man with an imposing Bavarian accent. "What would an ocean be without a monster lurking in the dark? It would be like sleep without dreams," my imagined feminine narrator would lilt. Why shouldn't she come off as equally profound?

A listener, when she realizes that she struggles to attend to only certain kinds of voices, apprehends the divisions in society. How we hear someone relates to that person's gender, race, sexual orientation, age, physical ability, and wealth. Some voices are perceived as authoritative, others are ignored; some are broadcast around the world, others fade for lack of funds. Attempting to create what the essayist Rebecca Solnit calls "a democracy of equal audibility" is a social enterprise— it's one of the tasks of feminist, antiracist, and economic justice movements. What would such a democracy sound like? Certainly not like one booming bass note.

The social prejudices that muffle other frequencies are often reinforced by those invested in the status quo. Some critics of the spirited, radical congresswoman Alexandria Ocasio-Cortez complain that she sounds like a teenage girl—as if that were such a terrible thing to be. Every time she speaks on the floor of the House of Representatives, Ocasio-Cortez helps to establish that higher-pitched voices can also be heard as commanding and capable. Greta Thunberg, a teenaged activist with Asperger's syndrome, similarly extends our auditory range. But Thunberg also points us toward another set of obstacles impeding our ability to hear. "Listen to the scientists," she often says. It's no accident that, for many people, listening to them has been difficult: fossil-fuel companies have spent millions to spread misinformation about climate change. To defend our right to listen to one another, we must sometimes strain to hear voices that the powerful would drown out.

* * *

Two years after the conclusion of his listening tour, Zuckerberg was questioned in Congress by Ocasio-Cortez. She noted that "the official policy of Facebook"—which declared during the lead-up to the 2020 election that it wouldn't ban ads that contain well-documented lies—"now allows politicians to pay to spread disinformation." She wanted to know how far this policy could be pushed. Would she, for example, be allowed to run ads falsely claiming that Republican candidates up for reelection had voted for the Green New Deal?

"Probably," Zuckerberg said. The previous week, he had delivered a lecture at Georgetown University titled "Standing for Voice and Free Expression." In it, he had placed his company in a lineage of free-speech pioneers, including Eugene Debs and Martin Luther King Jr. "The ability to speak freely has been central in the fight for democracy worldwide," he said. The central argument of the speech was that any attempt on Facebook's part to distinguish between deliberate disinformation and ordinary free speech would be antidemocratic.

How might Zuckerberg's rhetoric strike us if we also saw the ability of citizens to hear one another as central to democracy? From that perspective, the deliberate pollution of our common listening space might register as an antidemocratic act. The listening perspective is especially useful today, in the age of digital media. While Facebook and other social media platforms do facilitate speech, their business models revolve, in a fundamental way, around the manipulation and commodification of listening. We can shout into the social media void for free because what we say reveals valuable information about us; that information is then used to divide us into hyper-specific audiences. To maximize the effectiveness of the advertising targeted to those audiences, the platforms encourage certain kinds of attention more than others. A deluge of content and commentary—in which paid advertising, some of it political and deceptive, circulates alongside funny memes, awe-inspiring animal videos, and grassroots opinion—keeps us scrolling, conjuring the illusion of listening. But, by design, such feeds amplify the shallow, outrageous, and self-promoting, discouraging the prolonged engagement that deeper forms of listening require. The difference between the Facebook news feed and the debtors' assembly couldn't be more stark.

It can seem as though there's no principled way out of this conundrum: If you equate democracy with the proliferation of free speech, then how can you, in good conscience, restrict it? And yet—even setting aside the fact that social media platforms already manipulate the mix of messages we encounter—the history of thought about free speech does contain ideas that can be of use. Among them are the concepts of "audience interests" and the "right to hear," which have been repeatedly recognized by the Supreme Court. These concepts see the First Amendment from a listener's point of view. In addition to asking, "Do I have the right to speak," Genevieve Lakier, a professor at the University of Chicago School of Law, told me, we can ask, "am I, as a listener, genuinely hearing a diverse and representative array of views?"

The Supreme Court, Lakier has shown, took audience interests seriously during the New Deal era. In *Thornhill v. Alabama*, from 1940, it recognized a union's right to engage in peaceful picketing. The case was about free speech—the plaintiff, Byron Thornhill, was arrested while on the picket line—but the court's judgment addressed the importance of listening, too. One reason why the arrest was wrong, the justices concluded, was that citizens needed to hear what was being said: pickets could convey valuable information about working conditions, the causes of labor disputes, and how to regulate industry. In other First Amendment disputes from the period, Lakier said—including cases about pamphleting— the court furthered the cause of free expression by defending "the audience's right to have a diverse public sphere." Taking this right seriously entailed, inevitably, the consideration of economic disparities, so that what the court called the "poorly financed causes of the little people" might get a fair hearing.

These cases pointed in the direction of a democratic right to listen. But, today, audience interests are more likely to be invoked in defense of advertising or big political donors. In the infamous *Citizens United v. Federal Election Commission* decision, from 2010, which undid campaign-finance restrictions on free-speech grounds, the court looked to a 1978 opinion, *First National Bank of Boston v. Bellotti*, which argued that audiences had an interest in hearing what corporations had to say. In that opinion, the justices presaged, with uncanny precision, the click-maximizing ethos of the Facebook news feed: "The inherent worth of the speech in terms of its capacity for informing the public does not depend upon the identity of its source, whether corporation, association, union, or individual," they wrote. It's not too late to return to the more nuanced conception of audience interest that we used to favor. A revival of that older view might light the way toward a digital future in which meaningful democratic listening has a fighting chance.

* * *

In 2016, during one of the first shoots for *What Is Democracy?*, I stood near Miami Beach, asking people to share their political opinions on camera. Three middle-aged men on vacation from New Jersey sat down on a park bench to chat. They sang the praises of a Republican candidate for president named Donald Trump, and offered their thoughts about immigration (bad), taxes (too high), and police violence against Black people (not a problem). It was only a few minutes before one of them mentioned free speech. "Here, we have freedom to express," he said, of the United States. "Like when Joe was just explaining about his racism, six large Black men walked by. I thought there might be a problem. Not in this country! They heard it, it's democracy. Joe can say whatever he wants." What made America great, they suggested, was every individual's right to say anything, without reserve and without inviting a response. This was a conception of democratic life that centered on self-expression, with listening left out. In its version of democracy, speech need only go one way.

The men on the bench were hardly unique in overlooking listening as an important component of democracy. As an activist on the left, I long assumed that my role consisted entirely of raising awareness, sounding alarms, and deploying arguments. It took me years to realize that I needed to help build and defend spaces in which listening could happen, too. As citizens, we understand that the right to speak has to be facilitated, bolstered by institutions and protected by laws. But we've been slow to see that, if democracy is to function well, listening must also be supported and defended—especially at a moment when technological developments are making meaningful listening harder.

By definition, democracy implies collectivity; it depends on an inclusive and vibrant public sphere in which we can all listen to one another. We ignore that listening at our peril. Watching *What Is Democracy?* today, I find that the answer lies not just in the voices of the people I interviewed. It's also in the shots of people listening, receptively, as others speak.

11

THE INSECURITY MACHINE

Long before Covid-19 swept the globe, insecurity was already everywhere. Countless people faced housing, health, and food insecurity. Environmental insecurity was rising as changing weather patterns put communities at risk of fires and flooding. Prior to the advent of social distancing, we hid behind doors, locks, gates, and border walls, afraid of public space and one another. Online, we fretted over information security, devising passwords to access passwords, fearful we might be hacked or exposed. We were insecure at our jobs, in our homes, in our relationships, and on social media. We felt insecure about our very selves.

Given the ubiquity of insecurity, it may seem surprising that, only a few centuries ago, the word didn't even exist. A uniquely modern concept, *insecurity* first appeared in the seventeenth century. "Rather than being understood as an unalterable truth intrinsic to the human condition, 'insecurity' needs to be understood as the product of very specific historical circumstances," the political theorist Mark Neocleous

---

* Previously published as "The Insecurity Machine," *Logic Magazine*, no. 10 (May 4, 2020).

observes. Those particular historical circumstances were the rise of capitalism.

Consider the response to the coronavirus. In the United States, the devastation unleashed by this novel and dangerous pathogen has as much to do with economics as epidemiology. When whole sectors of the economy shut down to comply with orders to shelter in place, unemployment soared. Instead of paying workers to stay home to slow down the disease—a sensible, life-saving policy pursued in various ways by some wealthy countries, including Denmark—US officials handed trillions of dollars of public money to the world's biggest corporations. For the CEOs of these companies, the outbreak has been less a crisis than an opportunity. Not only did they receive a staggering no-strings-attached government handout, but they also have a more pliable and profitable workforce. When this pandemic passes, millions of people will be even more insecure and exploitable than they were at the outset. That will not be an accident.

Capitalism is an insecurity machine, though we rarely think of it as such. Alongside profits, commodities, and inequality, insecurity is a fundamental output of the system. Neither an incidental byproduct nor a secondary consequence of the concentration of wealth, it is one of capitalism's essential and enabling creations. "The bourgeoisie cannot exist without constantly revolutionizing the instruments of production, and thereby the relations of production, and with them the whole relations of society," Marx and Engels wrote in *The Communist Manifesto*, back when the most advanced machines were weaving cloth and harnessing steam. "Constant revolutionizing of production, uninterrupted disturbance of all social conditions, everlasting uncertainty and agitation distinguish the bourgeois epoch from all earlier ones." The beneficiaries of this arrangement dubbed it "creative destruction" before rebranding it as "disruption."

Our economic apparatus, in other words, destabilizes by design: market forces capsize communities and disintegrate old ways of life. Too often, however, we emphasize dramatic shifts, underscoring "great transformations" and systemic crises over comparatively quotidian developments, a temptation we must resist as we face the dual calamity of a global pandemic and an economic downturn. Engineered in order to facilitate exploitation and undermine solidarity, the production of insecurity is a daily phenomenon, its operations so commonplace as to appear banal. It is both physical and psychological: people endure inadequate housing, wages, and health care while our culture encourages self-blame and shame for financial hardship, relentlessly exploiting our fears and vulnerabilities. No advertisement will ever tell us we're OK and that it is the world that needs changing.

Of course, people have always lived precarious lives. Long before the industrial revolution, let alone the digital one, human existence was neither easy nor assured. This partly explains why *security*, unlike *insecurity*, is an ancient concept and aspirational ideal: etymologically, security comes from the Latin *securitas*, meaning freedom from worry, *sine cura*, or without care. In a similar fashion, commerce precedes capitalism. People have long engaged in the propensity to truck, barter, and trade. Capitalism emerges when the possibility of commerce becomes the necessity of competitive production. For that to happen— for market *opportunities* to become market *imperatives*—mass insecurity must be imposed and maintained.

Digital technologies provide new channels through which this process can unfold. Social media elevates paid advertising and sensational content, spreading misinformation and confusion, increasing epistemological insecurity. Data brokers create intimate profiles so that we might be better targeted— segmenting us into categories that include "rural and barely making it," "probably bipolar," and "gullible elderly"—while companies invest millions into "affect recognition" so they can figure out when we are most persuadable, increasing psychological insecurity. Opaque systems of information collection and predictive analytics facilitate new forms of discrimination and redlining, marking certain populations as criminal threats or directing them into subprime financial services, predatory mortgages, and exploitative rental markets, increasing housing insecurity. Employers monitor and control employees remotely, refusing to offer decent wages and benefits or provide consistent scheduling, increasing job insecurity.

Not everyone is made equally insecure by these tools, of course. That is precisely the point. The stability of ownership and investment for some necessarily depends on the destabilization and dispossession of others—and the struggle over housing and labor have always been the epicenters of this conflict. The spaces where we live and where we work are capitalism's main battlegrounds, and the rise of networked digital technologies have given capital more powerful weapons with which to conquer them—weapons we can be assured will be put to use as we enter a period of post-pandemic uncertainty and volatility.

* * *

In the summer of 2019, the residents of Atlantic Plaza Towers, a 718-unit apartment building in Brownsville, Brooklyn, got word that their landlord had plans to install a security system equipped with facial recognition. The devices would control entry to the twin high-rises and monitor all common areas.

The grounds were already covered in cameras. So who or what, exactly, would this new technology be making more secure? the tenants wondered. Contrary to the landlord's insistence that the devices were a "cool upgrade" that would keep keys out of the hands of the "wrong people," residents saw them as an unwelcome and unwanted intrusion—and one inextricably linked to a long and troubling history of racism, policing, and gentrification.

The mostly Black and female tenants were alarmed to learn of studies showing that facial recognition often perpetuates preexisting bias, with software most accurately able to assess men with white skin. They also worried about the collection of sensitive biometric data. "I'm afraid of it being shared with third-party agencies. I'm afraid of it being shared with the police. I'm afraid of it being shared with anyone—advertising companies, just everyone. It's just very sensitive information that I feel our landlord should not have," a young woman named Tranae Moran told the *Guardian*. Another resident, who had called the complex home for fifty-one years, was more blunt: "We do not want to be tagged like animals. We are not animals. We should be able to freely come in and out of our development without you tracking every movement."

One hundred thirty-four tenants filed a formal complaint. By banding together and partnering with lawyers, they thwarted the landlord's plan and made national news. Their success, however, represents more than a victory for privacy rights or the growing backlash against a particularly problematic technology. (Thanks to the work of activists, the use of facial recognition software by government agencies has been banned in a handful of US cities.) On a deeper level, the tenants identified and resisted one of capitalism's central dynamics: the fact that security for some is predicated on the insecurity of others.

While the landlord never said it directly, the protection of an investment, not the community, drove the adoption of the new camera system. Increased "security" was part of a bid to attract new, more affluent tenants, whose arrival would cause rents and property values to rise, threatening longtime residents with displacement. "He doesn't want Spanish. He doesn't want Black. He wants white people to come into the neighborhood," one tenant observed.

What happened in Brownsville is a variation of an old story, albeit with a high-tech twist. Property investments always involve what geographer Brett Story calls "the coercive scaffolding of enclosure and securitization," a scaffolding that harkens back to capitalism's murky origins in the English countryside. During the long and varied period called the enclosure movement, beginning in the twelfth century, wealthy landlords uprooted the peasantry in order to privatize once communal fields and forests, denying them their customary rights to the commons. A contemporary version of this dynamic now plays out in fast-gentrifying cities, where crime is redefined as a threat to the real estate industry's bottom line. Homeless people are the initial target, cleared off the streets by ordinances that outlaw panhandling or simply sitting on the sidewalk. Casting the poor not as residents deserving of respect and support but as miscreants on the wrong side of the law justifies their exclusion.

Nowhere is this more apparent, Story argues, than modern-day Detroit, where a coalition of real estate investors, including the billionaire founder of Quicken Loans, Dan Gilbert, are pushing forward a "revitalization" effort. As was almost the case in Brownsville, electronic monitoring plays a key role. In Detroit's downtown Chase Tower, a command center contains dozens of computer screens connected to approximately one thousand different outdoor cameras surrounding Gilbert's properties in seven states, which include over three hundred in metro Detroit alone. "The camera program is a collaborative effort that includes most of the big downtown property owners, including General Motors, Ilitch Holdings, and Compuware," Story writes, one that also coordinates closely with local law enforcement agencies. Dangling the prospect of economic growth, real estate moguls are able to redirect public power to private ends: the security guards that Gilbert employs can use force on civilians but are under no legal obligation to read detainees their Miranda rights.

In 1843, a young Marx described security—what he called "the concept of *police*"—as the "supreme concept" of bourgeois society. Fearful of those they have dispossessed, ruling elites have long utilized state violence to safeguard private assets, criminalizing both poverty and protest in the process. In 2016, Detroit's public-private surveillance system was used to track Black Lives Matter protesters. That same year, business owners formed a consortium called Project Green Light, which enabled them to stream their surveillance footage directly to city police facilities. "Now we don't have just one billionaire [doing it], we have five hundred businesses who pitch in and do their own areas," Detroit's mayor Mike Duggan boasted. Six months later, grassroots opposition successfully blocked the police department from using real-time facial recognition on Green Light's feeds, though the police continued to use the controversial technology in other ways.

* * *

Ever since Thomas Hobbes portrayed civilized men trading obedience for protection to escape a perilous "state of nature," security has been central to the liberal political tradition. Government, Adam Smith proclaimed, exists "for the security of property." Similarly, John Locke insisted that the reason men put "themselves under Government is the Preservation of their Property." Yet in Locke's view, not all property deserved to be preserved: he defended the British seizure of Indigenous territory in the Americas. The question, then as now, is *who* and *what* is being secured—and at whose expense.

Today, market logic so suffuses the concept of security that the term literally means property, like the security deposit you make before signing a lease or the securities owned by the affluent. It was these ironically named securities that brought down the global economy in 2008. Traders, using algorithms that coded Black borrowers and homeowners as particularly exploitable, gambled with securitized mortgages boasting inflated ratings. At the same time, the multibillion-dollar "lead generation" industry, which uses digital tools to compile and sell lists of prospective online customers, enabled lenders to identify potential subprime borrowers. This process, experts say, "played a critical, but largely invisible, role" in the mortgage crisis. In the end, nine million families saw their homes foreclosed on, wiping out half the collective wealth of Black families nationwide, further devastating deindustrialized cities like Detroit. With a few strokes of a keyboard, modern bankers caused dispossession on a scale that put the landowners of the original enclosure movement to shame.

The havoc wrought by the mortgage crisis in turn opened space for new algorithmically enabled land grabs. Invitation Homes, a private equity–backed firm, broke new ground by adopting machine learning systems to assess rental acquisitions, buying up huge swaths of property foreclosed during the subprime crisis on the wager that people would be willing to rent suburban houses they could no longer afford to own. One-fourth of single-family rentals belong to institutional investors, which have developed streamlined, smartphone-driven systems to manage them. Digital technology mediates all interactions between tenants and the company, from viewings to lease signings to repairs, inaugurating what scholar Desiree Fields calls the age of the "automated landlord." In March 2020, New York governor Andrew Cuomo tasked William Mulrow, a senior director at the private equity giant Blackstone Group, with spearheading the state's coronavirus economic recovery. Blackstone held a major stake in Invitation Homes until November 2019, when it sold its last shares for a total of around $7 billion.

As Fields has documented, the digital dimensions of this high-tech land grab go much deeper than a shiny interface. An assemblage of platforms and data analytics drives what the National Rental Home Council, a trade association, describes as "property management at scale." First, Invitation Homes' proprietary underwriting algorithm determines what properties the company should purchase by considering factors including "neighborhood desirability, proximity to employment centers, transportation corridors, community amenities, construction type, and required ongoing capital needs." Then networked technology allows investors to oversee large port-folios of far-flung units, with information quickly conveyed to capital markets so that additional money can be raised to expand the enterprise, while regular people who want to purchase a place to live are forced to compete with distant cash-rich investors working at digital speed. Hedge funds are happy to let buildings sit empty, waiting for them to appreci-ate, while locals pay the price.

Meanwhile, old biases persist and compound even when the platform is cutting-edge. Invitation Homes, for example, targets people of color who lack other housing options while charging them sky-high rates to meet Wall Street's outsized expectations. In other instances, opaque systems make dis-crimination difficult to prove. Automated decision-making enshrines socioeconomic disparities in an invisible, technical process, locking certain populations out or including them on predatory terms. One study from UC Berkeley found that, among online mortgage applicants, Black and Latinx borrow-ers paid over five basis points more in interest than white bor-rowers with similar financial backgrounds.

Racism is encoded in bad datasets and reinforced by the biases of disproportionately white, male, and privileged engi-neers—a process scholar Ruha Benjamin calls the "New Jim Code." In 2019, the Trump administration's Department of Housing and Urban Development implemented new rules effectively permitting automated discrimination in the hous-ing market, allowing algorithms to exclude and segregate on a landlord's or mortgage lender's behalf, setting a precedent of exempting digital technology from civil rights regulations. "It's going to drive people toward these algorithmic tools, and I think we'll end up in a marketplace where everyone is taking advantage of this loophole," Paul Goodman, a housing justice advocate, told *Dissent*. The powerful may soon be allowed to have computers mark certain populations as "risky" in order to dispossess them, and to do so without risking a lawsuit.

* * *

New technologies aren't just augmenting capitalism's insecurity-generating tendencies in the spaces that we call home. They are also intensifying those tendencies in the other domain that defines most of our lives: the workplace.

In early 2020 a friend regaled me with stories of working at a Brooklyn café. The place has a vintage and vaguely Parisian aesthetic—decidedly retro and low-tech. There are, of course, regulars, including a medievalist who likes to chat. On a slow day, another barista on duty was exchanging pleasantries with the medievalist when her phone rang: the owner was watching the security camera live feed from his laptop and told her to stop being so nice. When I asked my friend how many cameras are installed in the small space, she could identify at least eight and said there might be more. The charming café is, in fact, a panopticon—the boss can tune in anytime from anywhere and see from nearly every angle. The workers are always on edge, even when all they want to do is show a bit of kindness to a local eccentric.

As the scholar George Rigakos reminds us in his book *Security/Capital*, employers have been deploying cameras toward similar ends for decades. In the early 1990s, Rigakos worked at a bakery where the staff regularly took home broken and unsaleable loaves. Management had always looked the other way. But weeks before the business was scheduled to be closed, the owners installed security cameras to catch workers in the act. Lifelong employees were summarily fired, losing their retirement benefits. "The security cameras must have saved the company thousands upon thousands in severance and pension dollars," Rigakos recounts.

Today, employees no longer need to labor in the same physical space to be surveilled, nor is a human being required to do the surveilling. Instead, isolated and geographically dispersed, workers can be tracked and controlled remotely, whether they are driving for UPS or making deliveries for DoorDash or transcribing material for Rev. By harnessing digital technology, companies are able to offload more risk onto individuals, whom they categorize as independent contractors to bypass minimum-wage laws and other protections. A dwindling number of people are entitled to severance or pension dollars in the first place.

Work, we are often told, is becoming insecure. In reality, insecurity precedes work, or at least its waged variety. While some claim that insecurity is the inevitable consequence of innovation—the result of the fact that, as labor productivity rises, you need fewer workers to produce the same output— the fact is that people had to be *made* insecure, literally severed from their land and livelihoods, for capitalist working conditions to be foisted upon them.

Before the wage earner could emerge as our society's paradigmatic subject, the persona that we must all embody to survive, the condition of what historian Michael Denning calls "wagelessness" had to be imposed via the process of enclosure, after which peasants could no longer provide for themselves. "Capitalism begins not with the offer of work, but with the imperative to earn a living," Denning writes. Contrary to the

myth of liberal laissez-faire, employment relations are anything but natural, spontaneous, or freely chosen.

It wasn't until during the New Deal era that employment
became secure, at least for a subset of white men. During the
Great Depression, an unlikely assortment of social reformers,
radical workers, and "welfare populists" pushed to redefine
security as a social good guaranteed by the government. "For
a long time now people have been saying that perhaps the
greatest evil of capitalist industrialism is not its unequal distribution of wealth but the insecurity it brings to the majority of the population," the *New Republic* opined in 1935. If
capitalism was the problem, the Roosevelt administration's
solution was a robust welfare state. "Security" became FDR's
rallying cry.

In response, business went on the offense, embracing
the concept of security in order to redefine it. As historian
Jennifer Klein demonstrates in her 2003 book *For All These
Rights*, corporate elites devised a "firm-centered definition" of
security "in order to cultivate workers' loyalty to the company
and check the further growth of the welfare state." A full-time
job became more than just a paycheck—it was a lifeline to
unemployment benefits, retirement funds, and medical care.
Inadequate public programs left a gap that employers stepped
in to fill. Security was offered on an occupational as opposed
to universal basis.

The advent of neoliberalism in the 1970s and 1980s
marked the end of this arrangement. Corporate leaders
launched a concerted attack, breaking unions, reneging on
pensions, freezing wages, dodging taxes, and outsourcing jobs.
Determined to erode what remains of the New Deal compact, companies today strategically deploy digital technology

to shirk their end of the historic bargain. The development of AI-enabled labor-management systems undermine worker rights and safety through a combination of surveillance and predictive analytics, impacting everything from hiring to firing. Bots scan résumés and assess vocal intonation during job interviews, dictating who gets their foot in the door.

On the job, algorithms are harsh taskmasters, ranking and rating workers and automatically setting performance targets. Pickers in Amazon warehouses and shoppers for Instacart scramble to meet the demands of their digital overlords, enduring mental stress, chronic injuries, and even death. Unpredictable algorithmic wage cuts undermine economic stability, but they only come after a worker has been lured to a platform with promises of a living wage and "flexible" hours. Meanwhile, workers are kept in the dark, unable to understand or contest the decisions that set the terms of their lives and livelihoods.

For years, wannabe prophets predicted that robots were "coming for our jobs." That particular forecast, it turns out, has not come to pass. Instead, more and more people effectively have robots for bosses. Aggregating power in the hands of owners, managers, and developers, these digital systems secure profits by disregarding human beings' need for predictable incomes, schedules, and benefits—for security, in other words. When your supervisor is an algorithm, expect no remorse.

* * *

The powerful have never wanted the masses to be secure. The current crop of Silicon Valley overlords are hardly innovative in this respect. In the Middle Ages, Christian thinkers denounced security as a sin and an insult to God. "Perverse security," they called it. Today, tech billionaires are busy devising new sophisticated tools to spread insecurity so that they might become tomorrow's trillionaires.

Positioned to profit from mass precarity, they know that "disruption" is not a regrettable pit stop on the road to broadly shared prosperity, but a never-ending process that facilitates exploitation. Companies like Uber and Lyft benefit from the fact that millions of people can't make ends meet with one job; from the fact that rising housing costs mean a growing number of drivers have no choice but to live in their cars (many rent their vehicles from Uber, essentially turning them into app-controlled sharecroppers); and from the fact that most drivers are ashamed of their predicament, which makes them less likely to stand up for themselves. It's not a coincidence that homelessness tends to spike wherever the tech industry flourishes. The Bay Area's tent cities are symbolic of a digital economy that thrives on new forms of enclosure and dispossession.

Looking at capitalism through the lens of insecurity, as opposed to focusing solely on inequality, reminds us that people need more than higher pay; we need peace of mind and an ability to plan ahead. Strong regulations and robust public services are essential in this regard. Newly popular proposals, including national rent control and a homes guarantee that makes affordable housing a universal right, would have a socially transformative effect. In terms of labor rights, AB5, a California law that went into effect at the beginning of 2020 and classified drivers as employees rather than independent contractors, was an encouraging development. Clarifying the employment relationship would help stabilize people's incomes and lives. In response, Uber, Lyft, DoorDash, Postmates, and Instacart collectively spent a record-breaking $190 million to overturn it in a state-level ballot measure, Prop 22, which they strong-armed employees and misled the public into supporting.

But even if "independent contractors" were finally recognized as what they are—workers—that wouldn't be enough. The time has come to decouple security and employment, while also rethinking what security means in an age of ecological crisis and technological possibility. Indeed, the coronavirus outbreak has offered a distressing preview of the sort of upheaval climate change has in store. Overnight, millions of jobs evaporated and countless families were cut off from their medical coverage when they needed it most, laying bare the shortcomings of the New Deal settlement for all to see.

In contrast to the New Deal's individualistic and firm-centered conception of security, we need to devise a truly socialized security system, one predicated on universality and sustainability and geared toward redistributing not just wealth but risk. The frame of a Green New Deal moves us in this direction by centering collective solutions such as public housing, Medicare for All, and a federal job guarantee. The multitrillion-dollar stimulus package passed by Congress in the wake of the pandemic proves we have the money to pay for such policies, if only we can muster the political will.

Digital technology can and must be redirected to assist the cause—smart machines could help pair patients with physicians and improve their treatment, for instance, not target desperate customers with discriminatory insurance rates. But digital technology must also recede when appropriate. Leftists these days often say we need to decommodify, democratize, and decarbonize various realms of social life. We need to de-digitize many of them, as well.

Some technologies—think of the internet service providers we depend on for connectivity and the social media platforms we use to communicate, which have become even more essential to survival as people seek to physically isolate themselves—should be socialized and managed as public utilities. However, there are other technologies that shouldn't exist and plenty of data that shouldn't be collected. As tech critic Ben Tarnoff has argued, technology employed primarily for social control or to enforce austerity must be *abolished*, not democratized or socialized. The Atlantic Towers tenants were right—invasive facial recognition systems have no place in our communities—and they proved that popular mobilization can push back against harmful technology. Many more mobilizations will be needed to dismantle insecurity-generating algorithms in all of their forms, from biometric tracking in the workplace to behavioral targeting by advertisers.

Human beings will, of course, never be totally secure. The Stoic philosophers who first pondered the concept understood security as a psychological state, a kind of mental serenity that vulnerable, mortal, meaning-seeking creatures rarely feel. Two thousand years later, we live in a world where, though security on an existential level continues to elude us, economic security, or the fulfillment of everyone's basic needs, is feasible. And yet we inhabit a paradox: a new digital arsenal is being developed to ensure we remain insecure despite the abundance in our midst. Denied the basic resources we need to live, we are forced to seek security through market means—investing in ourselves as "brands," paying our insurance premiums, and praying that our retirement funds appreciate—while lining the pockets of those most responsible for making us insecure in the first place. Building a more secure world for everyone will be a challenge. But it's a risk we have to take.

12

THE DADS OF TECH

Coauthored with Joanne McNeil

"The master's tools will never dismantle the master's house," Audre Lorde famously said, but let Clay Shirky mansplain. It "always struck me as a strange observation—even the metaphor isn't true," the tech consultant and bestselling author said at the 2013 *New Yorker* Festival in a debate with the novelist Jonathan Franzen. "Get ahold of the master's hammer," and you can dismantle anything. Just consider all the people "flipping on the 'I'm gay' light on Facebook" to signal their support for marriage equality—there, Shirky declared, is a prime example of the master's tools put to good use.

"Shirky invented the internet and Franzen wants to shut it down," panel moderator Henry Finder mused with an air of sophisticated hyperbole. Finder said he was merely paraphrasing a festival attendee he'd overheard outside—and joked that for once in his *New Yorker* editing career, he didn't need fact-checkers to determine whether the story was true. He then announced with a wink that it was "maybe a little true." Heh.

---

* Previously published as "The Dads of Tech," *Baffler*, no. 26 (October 2014).

Shirky studied fine art in school, worked as a lighting designer for theater and dance companies, and was a partner at investment firm the Accelerator Group before turning to tech punditry. Now he teaches at New York University and publishes gung-ho tracts such as *Here Comes Everybody* and *Cognitive Surplus* while plying a consulting sideline for a diverse corps of well-paying clients such as Nokia, the BBC, and the US Navy—as well as high-profile speaking gigs like the *New Yorker* forum, which was convened under the stupefyingly dualistic heading "Is Technology Good for Culture?"

And that's tech punditry for you: simplification with an undercurrent of sexism. There are plenty of women academics and researchers who study technology and social change, but we are a long way from the forefront of stage-managed gobbledygook. Instead of getting regaled with nods and winks for "inventing the internet," women in the tech world typically have to overcome the bigoted suspicions of an intensively male geek culture—when, that is, they don't face outright harassment in the course of pursuing industry careers.

A woman interested in the digital transformation simply cannot inhabit the role of an avuncular, all-knowing figure ready to declare, definitively, whether technology is "good" or not. A female speaker is more likely to be asked if she knows how to code, the question implying she lacks the authority to comment on something as allegedly complex as the internet. Small wonder, then, that aspiring female leaders in the field are expected, like Sheryl Sandberg, to adopt a body of savvy solutions designed to retool their images so as to pose minimal threats to the boys' club—to "lean in" to the unfair expectations of a corporate culture that's often barely distinguishable from a frat party.

You need not be a mechanic or the designer of a highway system to comment insightfully on the impact of automobiles or problems with urban policy, of course. But where technology is concerned, guys like Clay Shirky get ahead on their looks—they look like authorities, like the kind of people who know how to build an iPhone app, though they themselves often don't have programming chops. Most prominent technology commenters are not coders—for the record, tech god Steve Jobs himself did not code—but that doesn't matter. They are men, so their competence upon opening their mouths is assumed. The master's tools are theirs.

* * *

"It's so easy even your mom can use it!" goes the common tech-marketing refrain. Dad's masculinity, the messaging implies, automatically ensures his grasp of all new products and services out of the gate. While women are belittled for (supposedly) not knowing how to use new tools, men are allowed to remain ignorant about the social context in which those tools are put to use and the fact that some people, and not only women, are prevented from using them. The result is *an internet so simple even your dad can understand it*, and it is this vision of the internet that dominates today; indeed, it is the vision presented by most men who make their livelihoods pontificating about technology. Complicated power dynamics do not fit neatly into an internet simple enough for Dad to understand. Instead, these unsubtle patriarchs believe the internet is a "neutral" device, "open" to any and all. Dad's simplified internet is a meritocracy, a place where the best rise to the top and competition makes regulation unnecessary. It is a realm where heroic innovators build on the work of their predecessors, steadily advancing and bettering humankind through the incessant upgrading of algorithms and apps, insistent that they are making the world more democratic and egalitarian even as they hoard wealth and influence for themselves.

Remember this: Whatever the cheerleaders of technological progress tell us, history does not move in a linear fashion. What feels like forward motion can suddenly stall out or reverse course, causing the loss of ground that once seemed securely held. Amid the endless stream of op-eds about how we need to get more girls into the male-dominated field of computer programming, few recall that, not long ago, leaders in the tech sector regarded it as a promising career choice for women. Grace Hopper, a legend in computer science, was part of the vanguard: she led the team that invented COBOL, a language that remains essential to data processing; received various honors throughout her career, including the Data Processing Management Association's "computer sciences man [sic] of the year" award in 1969; and coined the word *debugging* after clearing out a moth in a machine. "Women are 'naturals' at computer programming," Hopper told a *Cosmopolitan* reporter in 1967.

Nathan Ensmenger, author of *The Computer Boys Take Over*, has researched the advertising and recruiting efforts that effectively masculinized the industry. Computer companies in the late 1960s sought to elevate the prestige of programming by creating male-dominated professional associations and by portraying computer work as an analytical pursuit, more in the vein of chess than, say, plumbing. Ensmenger also found personality tests identifying the ideal programming type as someone with "disinterest in people." The image of the computer hacker as an antisocial, misunderstood genius—and almost invariably a dude—emerged from these recruitment efforts. And from there it was but a short step to the more benign, familiar, and materially successful ideal types of the Silicon Valley boy genius and the tech-savvy Dad that have helped mint hundreds of Clay Shirkys across the tech-seminar scene.

Indeed, the effort to transpose the gender profile of the computer industry was tightly bound up with a bid to enhance its class status, as had also been the case when professions such as medicine were aggressively masculinized. (You can chart a corresponding decline in class prestige when male-skewing professions, such as school teaching and psychotherapy, are feminized.) The leaders of the postwar computer industry took great pains to elevate the basic tasks of programming from their clerical office past and to equate them with rarified fields such as mathematics and logic. This concerted bid to deliver the industry into the analytical fingers of the "computer boys" affords a vivid contrast with the condition of the "telephone girls"—tens of thousands of young women entrusted to run the nation's communications network a century ago. At the outset of the telephonic revolution in communications, phone companies employed young men to operate the switchboards. The work was intellectually demanding, requiring technical knowledge of electricity to complete regular repairs, and physically exhausting. At some switchboard centers, workers placed an average of three hundred calls per hour.

When women flooded the field, the job itself did not change—women still had to handle and fix mechanical apparatuses. But the job *descriptions* changed; phone work was associated with "softer," stereotypically feminine interpersonal skills. Phone executives (who were exclusively men) considered women better suited for the task because they were less "unruly" than their male predecessors. Whereas programming gained esteem as an antisocial task, attracting lone and farseeing geniuses, the architects of the legacy technology of telephone switching denigrated their brand of service work as the opposite: an inherently social undertaking and thus more a labor of love than the hard job it actually was. It was, in short, "naturally" women's work.

Scholars have described telephone girls as "domestic machines," even though they were mostly young, unmarried women. And their consignment to the work ghetto of domesticity ensured that they'd be valued far more for the human connections they cultivated among the phone network's client base than for any mechanical contributions they made to the technology's advance. Just as the tech-savvy Dad is now the fallback image for technology's operations in the home, the stereotype of a terminally gadget-challenged Mom is a legacy of this deliberate division of labor hewed at the outset of the modern communications age.

Many official histories have written women out of the dominant narratives in both fields—computers and telephony. Scholars and popular authors alike tend to forget the earliest programmers, like Grace Hopper or the six women who worked at the University of Pennsylvania on one of the world's first electronic computers. Likewise, the general public has no sense of the impact women had on the development of telephony, envisioning them instead as ignorant and passive beneficiaries of a male-created, male-controlled tool. In reality, as Michèle Martin and other feminist historians point out, women not only ran the communications network, operating the switchboards as the pliant yet unseen phantoms in the machine, but also largely determined how the technology came to be used and, in two important ways, made it profitable.

At least one Bell Telephone manager went on the record crediting female employees with warding off insolvency: if the company had kept with the disobedient male operators, then it would have been "virtually facing bankruptcy." Women's influence as customers was even more profound. Though women had been initially a reviled demographic segment of a market designed by and for male business executives, they persisted in using the telephone for their own ends. Ultimately, they managed to repurpose the phone from a self-serious mode of business communication to the more casual instrument of sociability it is today. (Among other things, Martin observes, the habit of talking on the telephone for social "calls" allowed Victorian women to "visit" one another without having to put on time-consuming and constraining clothes.) Yet the ownership structure of the new technology ensured that women couldn't claim any share of the profits they helped generate: they may have made the phone appealing to the masses and put it to new use, but it was still the master's tool. Men owned the network.

When four hundred phone operators walked off the job, striking over harsh labor conditions and low wages in Toronto in 1907, and when, twelve years later, young women in Boston brought New England business to a halt by putting down their headsets to picket for better treatment and pay, they challenged common gender stereotypes that both their bosses and union leaders perpetuated. The latter group took umbrage at the idea of mere "petticoats" supplanting the traditionally male defenders of the working-class "family wage." (In some cities, women won concessions after shutting down the telephone system, but their victory helped convince owners they had to reduce their dependence on operators, so they rushed the automatic dial phone into service in order to render their restive female workforces obsolete.) Today, labor and management alike pay at least lip service to the ideal of equal opportunity, and women are officially welcome in workplaces and labor locals. Still, real gender parity in the house of labor remains an elusive ideal—and indeed, a retreating horizon in the tech and communications sectors.

*　*　*

The National Center for Women and Information Technology has reported that from 2000 to 2012, the proportion of first-year undergraduate women interested in majoring in computer science plummeted by 64 percent. For those who stick with their studies and find professional work, the attrition rate is just as dismal: 56 percent of women quit STEM (science, technology, engineering, and math) jobs by midcareer, a 2008 Harvard Business School study reported, which is double the number of men who quit. Demographic data confirms that economically and educationally privileged white men— "Dads," if you will—dominate Silicon Valley engineering and executive roles, which means they dictate who gets to join the team. Like devout upholders of high school hierarchy, entitled techies are notorious for alienating and excluding others only to justify their childish cliques with buzzwords like "culture fit"—which really just means "one of the guys."

The Dads of the internet may deny their complacency with structural inequality ("I'm not sexist, I have a daughter!"), but gender discrimination is as complex as any other lived experience. Neither perfect heroes nor villains exemplify the problem; hard evidence proves elusive or ambiguous when it comes to documenting the tech industry's pattern of discrimination. The high-profile case of Julie Ann Horvath, whose story made it all the way to the *New York Times*, may be emblematic. Her exit from GitHub, a popular website for collaborating on code, is not a straightforward narrative of gender bias, and it comes across as a puzzling, *Rashomon*-like saga to many tech observers who read about the case.

For one thing, the lines of direct authority are blurred—a not-uncommon occurrence in a tech scene dominated by start-ups committed to the paternalist image of the workplace as a family. In GitHub's case, the family talk appears to have been fairly literal and far from benign: much of the harassment and intimidation Horvath reports experiencing came from the wife of GitHub cofounder and former CEO Tom Preston-Werner, who was not an employee on the books but had power, influence, and clout at the company and appeared to target Horvath because she was one of the firm's few female employees. Preston-Werner himself, as the head of the company, is largely responsible for this mess, but a month after the story broke, GitHub posted a vague response that an internal investigation showed no "legal wrongdoing." He stepped down anyway, and the following week his GitHub cofounder Chris Wanstrath conceded that Preston-Werner had indeed "acted inappropriately," listing problems such as "confrontational conduct," "insensitivity to the impact of his spouse's presence in the workplace," and more.

Several other GitHub'ers were named as harassers, and Horvath claims her work was even erased because she turned down a date. In an email interview with *TechCrunch*, she described how a coworker who was "hurt from my rejection, started passive-aggressively ripping out my code from projects we had worked on together without so much as a ping or a comment. I even had to have a few of his commits reverted. I would work on something, go to bed, and wake up to find my work gone without any explanation." Instead of a traditional PR flack response, the counter to her claims, heavily circulated on tech blogs and Twitter, was a mudslinging Medium post from someone inside GitHub, concluding that this is a "story of the problems that arise when employees date coworkers and cannot separate work and personal life." Obviously the best way to challenge harassment allegations is with slut-shaming and anonymous cyberbullying.

The muffled windup of Horvath's case bespeaks a familiar pattern of subtle male managerial bids to undermine the career prospects and sap the confidence of women trying to climb the career ladder. Because she refused to defer to her harassers, Horvath endured regular questioning and scrutiny of her work product and her qualifications for her job as a developer. On *Slashdot* and Hacker News, commenters wondered how she got a job at GitHub in the first place and whether she could code at all.

Horvath's tribulations reminded many other women of their own experiences in similarly dicey environments. Ellen Chisa, then a product manager at Kickstarter, was among those inspired to speak out, posting an essay on her personal website titled "I'm Angry Because I'm Afraid." Chisa wrote that she admired Andreessen Horowitz, a venture capital firm that is one of GitHub's major backers. She went on to comment that she was "uncomfortable" when she saw the eponymous

Marc Andreessen expressing support for GitHub and Preston-Werner after news of the investigation broke. Andreessen is a billionaire who made a name for himself as cocreator of one of the first web browsers and who sits on the boards of companies including Facebook, eBay, and Hewlett-Packard, and though Chisa didn't couch her reflections as personal attacks, he went after her on Twitter. In a series of defensive replies, he fumed, "I expressed support for a founder, and you turned it into an accusation that I am hostile to women."

Chisa had not done anything of the sort—she had made the case that structural discrimination is impossible to ignore in the industry, especially when a public figure with "respect & weight in the community" like Horvath is a victim of it. Yet in Andreessen's twisted view, he was the one who had been wronged. The most affluent and influential speaker was the true injured party.

* * *

That a woman dared to call out sexism in the tech industry on a barely trafficked corner of the internet brought down the public wrath of one of Silicon Valley's most powerful men—the kind of man on whom many livelihoods and fortunes depend. Andreessen's Twitter-baiting attack on Chisa might seem, at first glance, like an isolated outburst by a thin-skinned egomaniac. Why else would a world-famous venture capitalist attack another company's project manager? But in fact, the whole exchange speaks volumes about the fraught intersection of technology and gender.

Women all over the working world face a disproportionate pushback when they stake out vocal positions in such controversies, but as this exchange illustrates, the pushback is

exceptionally virulent online (and when race, gender identity, and sexuality are added to the mix, retaliation can be
exponentially more malicious). Old bigotries and hierarchies
have carried over to new media with a vengeance. While early techno-utopians envisioned "cyberspace" as a place where
internet users could invent new selves, liberated from oppressive real-world constraints, internet discourse routinely, and
forcefully, transports women back into their offline bodies.
The virtual world, after all, is one endless exegesis of wom-
en's appearances (*What a hottie! What a cow!*). This seemingly
harmless chatter detracts from the content of a woman's con-
tribution to a conversation by focusing on her form. Much
more alarmingly, such talk is often a precursor to far more
menacing interactions, including the airing of rape threats
and death threats over infinitesimal disagreements.

Like other disadvantaged groups, women are subjected to
dehumanizing attacks; they're also offered unsolicited advice
from concerned gentlemen who instruct victims not to "feed
the trolls," convinced that the only proper and ethical way to
handle harassment is to ignore it, no matter how sinister or
disconcerting it may be. According to this commonly held
view, you must simply tune out tormentors, lest dudes aspiring to patriarch status find their First Amendment freedoms
vaguely abridged. As law professor Mary Anne Franks has
pointed out, this logic reveals a telling bias: freedom of speech
online, even if speech is harassing and hateful, is "really real"
and must be defended at all costs, while online harassment
is not "really real" and so does not need to be taken seriously.

The men who tell women not to feed the trolls are thinking
of an internet so simple that Dad can understand it. Though
keenly attuned to one form of injustice—the potential suppres-

sion of free speech—they cannot see other power dynamics at play, including the harms that result from virtual harassment (potential victims declining to participate in public forums, passing up speaking engagements and other opportunities for fear that violent ultimatums may not be empty threats, and so on). As they see it, women and others just need to "man up" and ignore the haters.

Analogous advice flows from Clay Shirky in a 2010 blog post titled "A Rant about Women," in which he blames the professional dominance of men on women's unwillingness to behave like "self-promoting narcissists, anti-social obsessives, or pompous blowhards . . . even when it would be in their best interests to do so." The link between self-promotion and advancement "isn't because of oppression," Shirky insists, "it's because of freedom." In a market society in which we are constantly competing and being ranked against each other, assertive people get noticed and opportunities logically follow. As well they should, Shirky continues, since "self-promotion is tied to other characteristics needed for success" and since male arrogance correlates with "chang[ing] the world."

Shirky believes that it's possible to decouple typically masculine self-aggrandizement from sexism, but that's because he assumes hubris is a neutral tool that women simply lack the will to effectively wield. In reality, the master's tools are kept off-limits to women, who, in myriad ways, are discouraged and penalized for picking them up. The master has many tricks up his sleeve to prevent the dismantling of his domain, including planting seeds of self-doubt (*If you don't know how to whittle and forge a hammer, how can you talk about the effect of nailing things?*), contending that women are actually holding the wrong tool (*That's not a hammer, it's a hair curler!*), or declaring women's work inferior even when presented with a row of perfectly hammered nails (*Let me show you how hammering is done, little lady!*). Even the master's rhetorical tools are off-limits, and this is what Shirky fails to comprehend: that a woman who follows his counsel and asserts herself or behaves arrogantly will be labeled pushy and punished for being a "bitch." Shirky can cheekily call his post a "rant," but women who argue emphatically risk being dismissed as overly emotional, as proven by the perennial disparagement of women as hapless, hysterical ranters—as unreliable and melodramatic no matter how accurate and rational they actually are.

From the trolls who terrorize minorities to billionaires who browbeat subordinates to commentators who maintain that the problem isn't misogyny but female cowardice, countless men insist that there is no such thing as sexism while upholding systems that exclude women. They continue to welcome abusers to the table, especially if they bring money, as was the case with Jeffrey Epstein, whose donations to the prestigious Media Lab at the Massachusetts Institute of Technology became the subject of scrutiny in 2019, though his predations had been long known. They want to believe in the myth of the internet as an even playing field, as an ideal and actually existing meritocracy, which means that if they are on top they deserve to be there—a gratifying and flattering thought. (The disgraced GitHub cofounder Preston-Werner used to work in a replica of the White House Oval Office with the words "United Meritocracy of GitHub" emblazoned on its rug.) Since the internet is open and there are no gatekeepers stopping women from going online, it must be an equal place. See? With that, voilà, all those old pesky social problems are resolved—feminism, at long last, can finally be over and done with, and civil rights can be something we celebrate as a historical triumph. The unexamined corollary of all this crackpot utopianism, though, is that if women programmers and executives fail to get ahead in the industry, the fault must be entirely their own—they're ill-disposed to coding, they don't design or delegate effectively, or they possess some other amorphous personal failing that's almost always a coy shorthand for neither white, male, nor "one of us."

Think of the vision of an internet so simple even Dad can understand it as a kind of imaginary map that pretends to describe reality as it instead delimits what's accepted as the natural and legitimate mode of interaction among male and female users and programmers in the tech world. Vintage templates trap us in a retrograde future: a full century after the telephone girls appeared, women still figure as domestic machines—as literally the master's tools. Two virtual personal assistant apps, named "Dawn" and "Donna," were inspired by female characters on television programs: "Dawn" for Don Draper's secretary on *Mad Men* and "Donna" for Donna Moss from *The West Wing.* The latter "proves herself invaluable by taking care of things and cleaning up messes before they happen," *TechCrunch* gushed. Blockbuster social networks like Facebook, Twitter, Tumblr, Foursquare, and Snapchat reliably reflect and perpetuate the values of the young men who started them. (Don't forget that an early-stage Mark Zuckerberg created a knockoff of the "Hot or Not" genre of frat-boy ogling to rank female students by attractiveness.) Lesser lights of the coding boys club tend to develop technologies to solve the trivial problems that beset their cohort—laundry and meeting girls—with apps like Washio and Down (previously named "Bang with Friends").

Venture capitalists love this stuff because they can understand it—because they are Dads. Paul Graham, cofounder of Y Combinator, a start-up incubator, sounded more like an Elite Models scout than a seasoned and savvy investor as he spelled out his corporate mission to the *New York Times*. He told the newspaper that "the cutoff in investors' heads [for start-up founders] is thirty-two" and said, "I can be tricked by anyone who looks like Mark Zuckerberg." Venture capitalists like Graham zero in on youth and appearance above talent. Like internet pundits who project authority by virtue of being pale-skinned, geeky, and middle-aged, these young men are also getting by on their looks. Indeed, data backs this up: a recent study from Harvard Business School proves that, consistently, "investors prefer entrepreneurial ventures pitched by attractive men." That's how the six-foot-five platitude-spouting egomaniac Adam Neumann managed to hustle investors out of billions of dollars for WeWork, a desk and office space renting shell game that came crashing down in early 2020 when bankers realized their payday was not guaranteed—not, as was well documented, because sexual harassment was endemic in the company.

No wonder, then, that investors ignore coders from marginalized communities who aspire to meet real needs. With an internet so simple even Dad can understand it as our guiding model, the myriad challenges that attend the digital transformation, from rampant sexism, racism, and homophobia to the decline of journalism, are impossible to apprehend, let alone address. How else could a white dude who didn't know that a "bustle" is a butt-enhancing device from the late nineteenth century raise $6.5 million to start a women's content site under that name? Or look at investors racing to fund the latest fad: "explainer" journalism, a format that epitomizes our current predicament. Explainer journalism is an internet simple enough for Dad to understand made manifest. Nate Silver's *FiveThirtyEight*, the *New York Times*' *The Upshot*, and *Vox* champion a numbers-driven model that does not allow for qualification or uncertainty. No doubt, quantification can aid insight, but statistics shouldn't be synonymous with a naive, didactic faith that numbers don't lie or that everything worth knowing can be rendered in a series of quickly clickable virtual notecards. Plenty of news reports cry out for further explanation, because the world is complex and journalists often get things wrong, but like internet punditry before it, these explainer outlets don't explain, they simplify.

* * *

In the current framework, the question posed by the *New Yorker* panel "Is Technology Good for Culture?" can be answered only with a yes or no—and plotted as it is along the binary logic of 1s and 0s, it chiefly serves to remind culture critics that the Silicon Valley mindset has already won. Though they appear to stand on opposite sides of the spectrum—unapologetic utopian squaring off against wistful pessimist—the Shirkys and Franzens of the world only reinforce this problem: things will get better or worse, pro or con. One reason we need to diversify the tech debate is to short-circuit this reductive polarity so we can imagine new questions, answers, and paths forward. For while men are free to adopt the ready-to-wear identities of futurist and nostalgist, no woman in her right mind can slip on such shopworn garb. Given the erosion of hard-won victories, especially in the realm of reproductive rights, there is no guarantee the future will be preferable to the present. Yet who would pine for a time when making coffee or taking dictation for these guys would have been a lucky break?

Audre Lorde herself pointed out that the master's tools may temporarily "beat him at his own game, but they will never enable us to bring about genuine change." Contrary to Shirky's point, people taking to Facebook to announce support for equal marriage rights may be one thing, but it isn't the same as Facebook hiring queer technologists or appointing queer board members, let alone considering diverse experiences in early product development. (Given that gay teenagers are rightfully scared that algorithms used by social media sites will inadvertently out them to their families, no one should mistake these platforms for the work of allies.) Hype about an Iranian "Twitter Revolution" in 2009 aside, Twitter was not designed to promote political change, nor was it conceived with concerns about trolls or stalkers in mind—like all other popular "free" online services, advertisers are its ultimate constituency.

In the end, an internet built by Dads, for Dads, sells most of us short. The stereotypical Dad, insulated from divergent perspectives, lacks the necessary understanding of how social problems and power inequities persist—and how these problems get amplified in a networked society. When we don simple-explainer goggles to survey a stubbornly unequal digital culture, every problem becomes black and white. Combating harassment becomes equivalent to state censorship of free speech, and web anonymity becomes "naturally" a straightforward issue: everyone should use their real names and have one identity online, because you shouldn't have anything to hide. After all, these Dads don't need to worry about being outed since they aren't sex workers or undocumented or disabled or vulnerable; nor are they activists or dissidents who need to worry about the National Security Agency.

Most of all, the dominance of the Dad's-eye-view of the world shores up the internet's underlying economic operating system. This also means a de facto free pass for corporate surveillance, along with an increasing concentration of wealth and power in the coffers of a handful of advertising-dependent, privacy-violating info-monopolies and the men who run them (namely Google and Facebook, though Amazon and Apple are also addicted to sucking up our personal data). Study after study shows that women are more sensitive to the subject of privacy than men, from a Pew poll that found that young girls are more prone than boys are to disabling location tracking on their devices to another that showed that while women are equally enthusiastic about technology in general, they're also more concerned about the implications of wearable technologies. A more complicated internet would incorporate these legitimate apprehensions instead of demanding "openness" and "transparency" from everyone. It would also, we dare to hope, recognize that the vacuous sloganeering on behalf of openness only makes us more easily surveilled by government and big business. But, of course, imposing privacy protections would involve regulation and impede profit—two bête noires of tech dudes who are quite sure that internet freedom is synonymous with the free market.

The master's house might have a new shape—it may be sprawling and diffuse and occupy what is euphemistically referred to as the "cloud"—but it also has become corporatized and commercialized, redolent of hierarchies of yore, and it needs to be dismantled. Unfortunately, in the digital age, like the predigital one, Dads don't want to take it apart.

13

THE AUTOMATION CHARADE

Somewhere, right now, a manager is intoning to a broke, exhausted underling that someone is willing to do the same job for less—or that some *thing* is willing to do it for free.

Since the dawn of market society, owners and bosses have reveled in telling workers they are replaceable. Robots lend this centuries-old dynamic a troubling new twist: employers threaten employees with the specter of machine competition, shirking responsibility for their avaricious disposition through opportunistic appeals to tech determinism. A "jobless future" is inevitable, we are told, an irresistible outgrowth of innovation, the livelihood-devouring price of progress. Sadly, the jobless future for the masses doesn't resemble the jobless present of the 1 percent who live off dividends, interest, and rent, lifting nary a finger as their bank balances grow.

Though automation is presented as a neutral process, the straightforward consequence of technological progress, one needn't look that closely to see that this is hardly the case.

* Previously published as "The Automation Charade," *Logic Magazine*, no. 5 (August 1, 2018).

Automation is both a reality and an ideology, and thus also a weapon wielded against poor and working people who have the audacity to demand better treatment, or just the right to subsist.

But if you look even closer, things get stranger still. Automated processes are often far less impressive than the puffery and propaganda surrounding them imply—and sometimes they are nowhere to be seen. Jobs may be eliminated and salaries slashed but people are often still laboring alongside or behind the machines, even if the work they perform has been deskilled or goes unpaid.

Remarkable technological changes are indeed afoot, but that doesn't mean the evolution of employment, and the social world at large, has been preordained. We shouldn't simply sit back, awestruck, awaiting the arrival of an artificially intelligent workforce. We must also reckon with the ideology of automation and its attendant myth of human obsolescence.

* * *

This myth of human obsolescence was on full display when elites responded to the initial campaigns of the Fight for 15 movement. As exploited and underpaid fast-food workers went on strike across the country in 2013, agitating for little more than a livable wage, pundits scoffed that the protests would only spur employers to adopt fleets of burger-flipping robots. The Employment Policies Institute, a conservative think tank, took out a full-page ad in the *Wall Street Journal* to drive this message home—and presumably to persuade disenchanted food-service workers that they were lucky to have a job at all: "Today's union-organized protests against fast food restaurants aren't a battle against management—they're a battle against technology. Faced with a $15 wage mandate, restaurants have

to reduce the cost of service in order to maintain the low pric-
es customers demand. That means fewer entry-level jobs and
more automated alternatives—even in the kitchen."

Former McDonald's CEO Ed Rensi got plenty of press attention when he expressed similar sentiments. "It's not just
going to be in the fast food business," Rensi said. "If you can't
get people a reasonable wage, you're going to get machines
to do the work. . . . And the more you push this it'll just
happen faster." Employers, he continued, should actually be
allowed to pay certain groups—high school kids, entry-level
workers—even less than the meager amount they currently
get thanks to the floor set by federal minimum-wage law.

Soon after making these remarks, Rensi provided gloat-
ing commentary for Forbes.com that his warnings about
automation had already proven true. "Thanks to 'Fight for
$15' Minimum Wage, McDonald's Unveils Job-Replacing
Self-Service Kiosks Nationwide," boasted the headline.
Rensi could barely contain his glee—though he did gamely
try to shed a few crocodile tears for the burger behemoth's
now-redundant corps of line workers. "Earlier this month,
McDonald's announced the nationwide roll-out of touch-
screen self-service kiosks," Rensi wrote. "In a video the company released to showcase the new customer experience, it's
striking to see employees who once would have managed a
cash register now reduced to monitoring a customer's choices
at an iPad-style kiosk."

In reality, what is actually striking when you watch that video
is not the cybernetic futurism but rather just how unautomated
the scene is. Work has not disappeared from the restaurant floor,
but the person doing the work has changed. Instead of an employee inputting orders dictated by the customer, customers now

do it themselves for free, while young, friendly-looking employees hover nearby and deliver meals to tables.

Rensi certainly had grounds to gloat—what mercenary corporation wouldn't want to substitute paid staff with people who pay for the privilege of doing the work needed to keep the company afloat? But to grace this latest move toward the casualization of low-skilled service work with the somber moniker of "automation" exponentially oversells the shifting workplace dynamic. McDonald's customers aren't on the brink of some hyper-digitized foray into commerce that we might recognize from sci-fi fare like *Minority Report* or *Black Mirror*. Instead, they're, if anything, on course to re-experience the rather quaint dining chambers of the midcentury automat.

Hence, I propose making our idea of automation itself obsolescent. A new term, *fauxtomation*, seems far more fitting.

* * *

In its more harmless form, fauxtomation is merely a marketing ploy, a way to make pointless products seem cutting-edge. The Tovala "smart oven," for example, is Wi-Fi-connected and scans barcodes to glean reheating instructions for premade meals available through a subscription delivery service. Overpriced TV dinners cooked in an expensive toaster hardly live up to the slogan "Cook your own ingredients with your smartphone."

The gap between advertising copy and reality can be risible. But fauxtomation also has a more nefarious purpose. It reinforces the perception that work has no value if it is unpaid and acclimates us to the idea that one day we won't be needed.

Where Hollywood's sci-fi futurism and leading tech pundits lead us astray, however, socialist feminism can lend invaluable insight, inoculating us against techno-capitalism's self-flattering claims. The socialist feminist tradition is a powerful resource because it's centrally concerned with *what work is*—and in particular how capitalism lives and grows by concealing certain kinds of work, refusing to pay for it, and pretending it's not, in fact, work at all.

That women have special insight into technology shouldn't come as a surprise: after all, they have been sold the promise of liberation through laborsaving devices since the dawn of mass consumerism, and this applies to kitchen appliances in particular. (It's a short and rather sad leap from self-cleaning ovens to self-cooking ones.) Despite this, they have seen their workloads multiply, not diminish.

In her study *More Work for Mother: The Ironies of Household Technology from the Open Hearth to the Microwave*, Ruth Cowan sheds astonishing light on the way innovations like electric irons and vacuum cleaners only added to the list of daily chores for women confined in the cult of domesticity. These innovations also increased cleanliness standards—that is, ramped up the productivity expectations for home workers as well as their workloads—while transforming housekeeping into a more gendered, solitary, time-consuming occupation. Here is an especially vivid reminder from our patriarchal past that automation isn't all it's cracked up to be, and hardly guarantees the absence of work.

But the relevant critique here runs deeper than simply observing that better living through technology was often an empty publicity slogan. Socialist feminists have long argued that women have been fed a lie—a lie that is increasingly foisted on the entire population, regardless of gender: they have been told their labor is not worthy of a wage and thus has no social value.

The Italian theorist Silvia Federici has tenaciously analyz-
ed the ways in which feminized, domestic work—what she
calls reproductive labor—is essential to capitalism even as capitalists and bosses refuse to acknowledge its productive existence. Beginning with her activism with the group Wages for
Housework in the 1970s, Federici has argued that we must recognize the underappreciated, uncompensated labor that sus-
tains everyday life, providing the foundation that underpins
all manner of paid work recognized by the formal economy.
Every bridge, every factory, every Silicon Valley app is merely
the visible tip of a hidden iceberg of reproductive labor.

It's an insight that may seem obvious, but is actually revelatory. At the University of Toronto in 2017, I watched as
Federici fielded an earnest question from a graduate student
who said something about how automation would expand
the reserve army of labor—Karl Marx's term for the multitude of workers without access to steady employment. The
graduate student took for granted that, soon enough, there
would not be enough work to go around and that many people would become surplus, expendable, and effectively irrelevant to society. Many in the audience nodded their heads in
agreement—including me.

Federici's response was bracing. She vehemently denied the
premise of the question—that we must acquiesce to the idea
that, come the great automated apocalypse, masses of people would have no productive work to do: "Don't let them
make you think that you are disposable," she passionately proclaimed. At that moment, I realized the depth of Federici's
insight. Her point is not that women have, historically, per-
formed reproductive labor outside the sphere of waged work,
that their efforts are supplemental to the real action. Rather,

she insists that reproductive labor is utterly central: in its absence, the entire system would collapse.

The joint creation of social life is the very basis of all economic activity. There would be no gross domestic product to contribute to without it, no assets to leverage or profits to hoard. We are more important and powerful than we have been led to believe—and the *we* in question here is no longer just the marginalized ranks of women performing reproductive labor, but increasingly the postindustrial precariat at large.

* * *

As socialist feminism usefully highlights, capitalism is dedicated to ensuring that as much vital labor as possible goes uncompensated. Fauxtomation must be seen as part of that tendency. It manifests every time we check out and bag our own groceries or order a meal through an online delivery service. These sorts of examples abound to the point of being banal. Indeed, they crowd our vision in virtually every New Economy transaction once we clue into their existence.

One afternoon I stood waiting at a restaurant for a to-go meal that I had ordered the old-fashioned way—by talking to a woman behind the counter and giving her paper money. As I waited for my lunch to be prepared, the man in front of me appeared astonished to receive his food. "How did the app know my order would be ready twenty minutes early?" he marveled, clutching his phone. "Because that was actually me," the server said. "I sent you a message when it was done."

Here was a small parable of labor and its erasure in the digital age. The app, in its eagerness to appear streamlined and just-in-time, had simply excised the relevant human party in this exchange. Hence the satisfied customer could fantasize that his food had materialized thanks to the digital interface, as though some all-seeing robot were supervising the human workers as they put together his organic rice bowl.

Our general lack of curiosity about how the platforms and services we use every day really work means that we often believe the hype, giving automation more credit than it's actually due. In the process, we fail to see—and to value—the labor of our fellow human beings. We mistake fauxtomation for the real thing, reinforcing the illusion that machines are smarter than they really are.

Though omnipresent, fauxtomation can sometimes be hard to discern, since by definition it aims to disguise the real character of the work in question. *The Moderators*, a moving 2017 documentary directed by Adrian Chen and Ciaran Cassidy and released online through the Field of Vision series, provides a rare window into the lives of individual workers who screen and censor digital content. Hundreds of thousands of people work in this field, ceaselessly staring at beheadings, scenes of rape and animal torture, and other scarring images in order to filter what appears in our social media feeds.

If what we encounter on Facebook, OkCupid, and other online platforms is generally "safe for work," it is not because algorithms have sorted through the mess and hidden some of it from view. Rather, we take non-nauseating dips in the digital stream thanks to the labor of real-live human beings who sit before their own screens day and night, tagging content as vulgar, violent, and offensive. According to Chen, more people work in the shadow mines of content moderation than are officially employed by Facebook or Google. Fauxtomatons make the internet a habitable place, cleaning virtual public squares of the sort of trash that would chase most of us offline and into the relative safety of face-to-face interaction.

Today many, though not all, of the people employed as content moderators live abroad, in places like the Philippines or India, where wages are comparatively low. The darkest tasks that sustain our digital world are outsourced to poor people living in poorer nations, from the environmentally destructive mining of precious minerals and the disposal of toxic electronic waste to the psychologically damaging effects of content moderation. As with all labor relations, race, gender, and geography play a role, determining which workers receive fair compensation for their labor or are even deemed real workers worthy of a wage at all. Automation, whether real or fake, hasn't undone these disturbing dynamics, and it may well intensify them.

* * *

For many, the concept of fauxtomation may conjure the famous image of the Mechanical Turk, a fanciful eighteenth-century contraption that purportedly knew how to play chess. (In truth, the Turk was an elaborate hoax with a human player hidden under its board.) Amazon adopted the Turk as its mascot to advertise its crowdsourcing service, Amazon Mechanical Turk, which enables an enormous distributed workforce to perform piecemeal tasks for less than minimum wage even though most "turkers" reside in the United States. (Automation cheerleaders like Rensi must be crushed that no app has yet figured out how fries can be bagged from afar.) Amazon's cheeky slogan—"artificial artificial intelligence"—acknowledges that there are still plenty of things egregiously underpaid people do better than robots.

But a better predecessor for fauxtomation as I understand it would be Thomas Jefferson's dumbwaiter—which, if it were invented today, would probably be called the "smartwaiter," in keeping with Silicon Valley's intelligence-fetishizing argot. Jefferson is hailed as a great American thinker and tinkerer. But he also, arguably, deserves credit as the first great American fauxtomator. His legendary estate, Monticello, was full of ingenious devices.

Jefferson did not invent the dumbwaiter himself, but was an avid user, as Monticello's website makes clear: "The dumbwaiters—some of which were built at Monticello—were on casters so that they could be wheeled to the table. A guest who dined at the President's House during Jefferson's tenure recalled: 'by each individual was placed a dumbwaiter, containing everything necessary for the progress of dinner from beginning to end.'"

A YouTube video produced by the Thomas Jefferson Foundation goes into greater detail, showing exactly how the historic devices worked. As we're encouraged to marvel at the dumbwaiter's quaint design, a gentle voiceover struggles to adequately grapple with the cruelty behind Jefferson's contraptions:

> In Jefferson's dining room, he installs dumbwaiters into both sides of the fireplace mantel. A weight drops, and a bottle rises from the wine cellar directly below the dining room. Just outside the dining room is a revolving door with shelves on it, so when the food is ready to serve, it can be brought upstairs, loaded on the shelves, and the door turned into the room. These gadgets impress visitors, but they also allow Jefferson to hide something from his visitors, and that is the reality of slavery. . . . One of Jefferson's

own visitors noted these things that Jefferson was doing—noted Jefferson's conversations about what he called "ameliorating slavery," as though it could be made better—and her observation was simply this: that Jefferson was doing nothing more than gilding the chains of slavery.

Jefferson gilded chains by making them hard to see. Enlaved people ("members of the enslaved community" as the video awkwardly dubs them) cooked hot food and put it on shelves, making it appear as if the evening's fare had been conjured by magic. The same hidden hands whisked away dirty plates just as quickly. Enslaved people also stood at the ready in the basement, waiting to load up any wine the master and his guests required. The appearance of seemingly automated abundance Jefferson so doggedly cultivated required substantial additional labor—the labor of making labor seem to disappear.

More than 150 years later, Black workers in Detroit toiling at what were widely regarded as the nation's most secure and iconic jobs—the automobile assembly line—called out another form of false innovation. In 1968, radical organizer and editor John Watson decried the prevailing and degrading situation of "speedup, bad working conditions, automation," in which "one black man does the job previously done by three white men." According to Detroit icon and activist Grace Lee Boggs, members of the United Auto Workers, including her husband, Jimmy Boggs, used the term "man-o-mation" to describe the dynamic.

As Dan Georgakas and Marvin Surkin make clear in *Detroit: I Do Mind Dying*, workers had good reason to poke holes in employers' high-tech pretense: "In 1946, some 550,000 auto workers had produced a little more than three million vehicles, but in 1970 some 750,000 auto workers had produced a little more than eight million vehicles." The rapid pace took a devastating toll of people's health and lives, leaving millions of workers disabled or dead; one study from the period estimated "sixty-five on-the-job deaths per day among autoworkers." Auto industry executives credited the industry's productivity boom to advances in machinery, but the predominantly Black workforce knew it was in fact due to old-fashioned exploitation, not automation: heavier work-loads and unsafe, unhealthy conditions.

* * *

Over two thousand years ago Aristotle dreamed of a self-weaving loom that would end slavery and exploitation. In the eighteenth and nineteenth centuries the Luddites broke weaving machines in protest against the domination and destitution that came with the new contraptions, only to be unfairly remembered as opponents of progress. Today, in our own optimistic reveries about laborsaving devices, we too often forget to ask, Who owns the looms?

There is no denying that technological possibilities that could hardly be imagined a generation ago now exist, and that artificial intelligence and advances in machine learning and vision put a whole new range of jobs at risk. Entire industries have already been automated into nonexistence: Kodak was decimated by digital photography and Instagram, Netflix and Amazon killed off Blockbuster, and ATMs made countless bank tellers obsolete.

The problem is that the emphasis on technological factors alone, as though "disruptive innovation" comes from nowhere or is as natural as a cool breeze, casts an air of blameless inevitability over something that has deep roots in class conflict. The phrase "robots are taking our jobs" gives technology agency it doesn't (yet?) possess, whereas "capitalists are making targeted investments in robots designed to weaken and replace human workers so they can get even richer" is less catchy but more accurate.

Capitalism needs workers to be and feel vulnerable, and because automation has an ideological function as well as a technological dimension, leftists must keep intervening in conversations about technological change and what to do about it. Instead of capitulating to the owning class's loose talk of automation as a foreordained next phase of production, we should counter with demands that are both visionary and feasible: a federal job guarantee that provides meaningful work to all who want it or job sharing through a significant reduction in the workweek. When pundits predict mass unemployment following a robot takeover, we should call for collective ownership of the robots and generous social benefits detached from employment status, including pushing for a progressive variation of a universal basic income under a rallying cry that updates the 1970s socialist feminist slogan to Wages for *All* Work—not just the work that bosses recognize as worthy of a meager paycheck.

We have to recognize both the dangers and possibilities associated with automation while relentlessly poking holes in rhetoric that seeks to conflate technology's present and potential capacities with an inescapable, and deeply exploitative, way of organizing labor and compensation. Where fauxtomation attempts to pass as automation, we should call it out as such.

Of course capitalists want working people to be precarious, pitted against one another, and frightened about what the future may hold. Of course they want us to think that if we dare to push back and demand more than scraps the robots will replace us—that we can be automated away at the push of a button. They may wish that were the case and are no doubt investing their fortunes toward making it seem so. But it, and indeed anything like it, has not come close to being true. If the automated day of judgment were actually nigh, they wouldn't need to invent all these apps to fake it.

14

WHO SPEAKS FOR
THE TREES?

On the corner of South Finley and Dearing Streets in
Athens, Georgia, the small college town where I grew
up, there is a tall white oak, and a small weathered stone
plaque that reads,

> For and in consideration of the great love I bear this tree
> and the great desire I have for its protection, for all time, I
> convey entire possession of itself and all land within eight
> feet of the tree on all sides.
>
> —*William H. Jackson*

The Tree That Owns Itself is a beloved local landmark, one
I visited many times as a child. Standing under its branches
provoked a subtle awe, a respect not usually granted to mere
plants. The tree was imbued with rights, not an object but a
subject, animate, existing with a kind of inviolability and autonomy. It had also achieved that elusive quality that so many
self-possessing humans desire: fame.

---

* Previously published as "Who Speaks for the Trees?," *Baffler*, no. 32
(September 2016).

The tree got its first taste of notoriety in a front-page *Athens Weekly Banner* article published on August 12, 1890, under the headline "Deeded to Itself," although in truth, the tree had been in self-possession for more than half a century by that time. Another half-century after the *Banner* article was published, the original oak, so beloved by Mr. Jackson, fell after an unusually strong storm. The community rallied to plant a seedling cultivated from one of the tree's acorns; the new oak has thrived in the same plot since 1946. Thus, as noted on another small plaque, the Tree That Owns Itself is technically "the scion" of the initial Tree That Owns Itself. Nevertheless, the Scion of the Tree inherited its parent's unusual claim to independence. This claim is not necessarily binding, because Georgia common law, like that of all other states, does not recognize the capacity of trees to hold property, since plants, like nonhuman animals, have the legal status of things and thus lack the right to have rights. Yet the tree's self-possession is an accepted part of local identity and lore and has never been challenged in court. In the minds of Athenians, the tree owns itself and its plot.

Perhaps in the near or distant future, the Tree That Owns Itself will not be regarded as a charming curiosity but as a political pioneer, the embodiment of an imaginary and ethical leap that foreshadowed what will seem, from the future's transformed vantage point, the inevitable and necessary expansion of rights to the natural world. In 1972, law professor Christopher Stone provided a sketch of what such a future might look like in a groundbreaking scholarly essay, written on a whim after he found himself arguing "the unthinkable" in a class lecture. Still widely read more than forty years later, *Should Trees Have Standing?* doesn't go so far as to contend that all flora should be given a deed to the soil in which they are planted (like our arboreal outlier in Athens) but it does systematically and dispassionately make the case for granting baseline "legal rights to forests, oceans, rivers, and other so-called 'natural objects' in the environment—indeed, to the natural environment as a whole."

It's not as strange as it may sound, for the uncanny entity that is the nonhuman "person" is already omnipresent. "The world of the lawyer is peopled with inanimate rights-holders: trusts, corporations, joint ventures, municipalities, Subchapter R partnerships, and nation-states, to mention just a few," Stone reminds us. Corporations were granted legal personhood in 1886—and oddly, it happened in an almost backhanded way. The Supreme Court did not directly rule on the matter. In a headnote that wasn't part of the formal opinion in *Santa Clara County v. Southern Pacific Railroad Company*, the court reporter (who had sympathies with the railroads) noted that chief justice Morrison Waite affirmed the personhood of corporations under the Fourteenth Amendment in a passing comment as proceedings began. Of course, railroad attorneys and business interests had been opportunistically demanding for years that the "equal protection" clause of the amendment designed to secure equal rights for former enslaved people be twisted to apply to corporations. The *Santa Clara* trial affirmed their Gilded Age aspirations as fact, even though the suit was decided on other grounds: "defendant Corporations are persons within the intent of the . . . Fourteenth Amendment." Later cases built on that thin precedent. Today, corporations are entitled to an ever-expanding array of constitutional protections, from the Fourth Amendment ban on warrantless search and seizure to the First Amendment guarantee of free speech.

"Convincing a court that an endangered river is 'a person,'" Stone acknowledges, "will call for lawyers as bold and imaginative" as Southern Pacific Railroad's counsel—and, one might add, considerably less mercenary. That's because extending rights to other forms of nonhuman life entails fighting to counteract the rights of corporations and the remarkable power personhood allows profit-seeking ventures. The intrepid lawyers and citizens who have taken up this gauntlet challenge our legal and economic systems, while chipping away at the moral framework of human separateness and superiority that has evolved and solidified over millennia.

* * *

Grant Township is a tiny community of seven hundred citizens that sits in Indiana County in western Pennsylvania. Should you drive through, you might not realize you were there: it boasts no downtown, no stores, no traffic lights, no public sewage, and few jobs. But there is land and water, and there are trees and animals, king among them the eastern hellbender, North America's largest aquatic salamander—and all of this natural richness is vested with rights. According to a Community Bill of Rights Ordinance issued June 3, 2014, and adopted by the residents, "Natural communities and ecosystems within Grant Township, including but not limited to, rivers, streams, and aquifers, possess the right to exist, flourish, and naturally evolve." With a single vote they became rights-holding entities, potential legal persons.

Grant Township adopted this ordinance as a direct challenge to the Pennsylvania General Energy Company (PGE), which wanted to create a seven-thousand-foot "class II" injection well within the township's border, pumping fracking waste into empty boreholes. That toxic fluid threatens to seep through rock formations into local aquifers, poisoning drinking water and ecosystems with hazardous chemicals and radioactive materials. More than one hundred communities in Pennsylvania have taken the unusual step of embracing some version of the same Community Bill of Rights, including rights for the environment, to oppose various kinds of polluters, but Grant Township has taken the struggle farther than most. They have done so, township supervisor Stacy Long told me, not because they are a bunch of Gaia-worshipping hippies but because they have run out of options—at least within the boundaries of the law as it is written.

Like many battles, Grant Township's began with a bureaucratic formality. In August 2013 a small notice appeared in the local paper saying the Environmental Protection Agency was hosting a public hearing about the planned well. On the scheduled evening, EPA officials stood shoulder to shoulder with gas company representatives and assured residents all would be fine. The residents, knowing better, had come to the hearing prepared, naively assuming their research and reasoned arguments about the dangers inherent to the project would prevail. It quickly became evident that the EPA, failing to live up to its name, intended to rubber-stamp the plans. At a later meeting with township supervisors, PGE employees were blunt: the state has complete authority in these matters; the township has no say; we are going forward with the well whether you like it or not. "We had no leverage," Long told me. "We were sitting ducks." For the people of Grant Township, disillusionment morphed into open rebellion.

* * *

Like it or not, PGE was fundamentally correct. The law was indeed on the utility's side, representatives of the Community Environmental Legal Defense Fund (CELDF), a nonprofit law firm, confirmed when Long and others connected with them. Once permits were secured, disposing of hazardous materials on property abutting people's homes was the corporation's right. It didn't matter that in 2014 a Government Accountability Office report found that, as a consequence of underfunding, the "EPA is not consistently conducting two key oversight and enforcement activities for class II programs"; it didn't matter that an earlier investigation by the journalism nonprofit *ProPublica* found that the EPA didn't know how many wells existed or the volume of waste pumped into them and that it failed to keep the records required by the Safe Drinking Water Act; it didn't matter that many scientists have warned about the potential dangers of injection wells due to "waste migration" and water contamination; it didn't matter that PGE, one of the state's top polluters, had a history of environmental violations; it didn't matter that injection wells have also been linked with earthquakes in Ohio, Oklahoma, and Texas. The only recourse, CELDF explained, was for Grant Township to change the rules of the game, to tilt the playing field in the residents' and ecosystem's favor. That's what the township did by implementing the Community Bill of Rights.

According to CELDF organizer Chad Nicholson, the fundamental issue is less environmental than political: "It's about who has more rights, who has the authority to legislate and make decisions." Community control may not be desirable in many cases—if a suburb wanted to segregate its schools, say—but state and federal laws also do things like block towns from protecting the health and safety of residents, and that's what

CELDF's ordinances are designed to challenge. The group's radical, rights-based approach is relatively new. Beginning in 1994, CELDF was a conventional environmental law firm, working with communities to painstakingly appeal industrial permits. CELDF attorneys would often win the first round, perhaps having identified some clerical error or deficiency in the application and would celebrate over a beer, but the company would eventually successfully resubmit. Though it won accolades, including from the White House, the organization had an existential crisis. "The bitter irony," Nicholson explained, "is that we were helping corporations build better permits and helping the corporate lawyers, who got to bill another round while the company got to write off the expense."

Predictably, PGE wasted no time in suing Grant Township, asserting that the Community Bill of Rights ordinance was unconstitutional and in violation of the corporation's rights under the First and Fourteenth Amendments, in addition to the Commerce and Supremacy Clauses of the US Constitution. A judge found that the municipality had indeed exceeded its authority. The ruling stripped out most of the ordinance, including the rights of nature—which only caused the town to escalate the rebellion. Within weeks, a majority of the residents voted in a "home rule charter," essentially changing their local form of government to override the judge and reinstate their Bill of Rights. In the interim, CELDF had the local watershed—the Little Mahoning Watershed, which includes a 4.3-mile stretch of stream that is home to fish, freshwater mussels, aquatic insects, and the aforementioned hellbender salamander—join a motion to intervene in PGE's lawsuit, seeking to "defend its legally enforceable rights to exist and flourish."

The Grant Township residents I spoke to were aware of the risks they were taking. If the litigious watershed lost the case, the community could face millions of dollars in damages and legal fees and possible bankruptcy. Long, who as a supervisor has access to the books, assured me that the township has no wealth or real tax base. "What are they going to do?" Long asked. "Take our garbage? Our public sewage? We don't have either. We don't have anything to give." And that, she continued, is why PGE came to them in the first place—because the township's citizens are poor. "Rural areas like ours are the sacrifice zones for the gas industry."

By fighting back, the township has resisted such a fate. After five years of legal maneuvering and relentless intimidation tactics from their opponents, a stunning reversal occurred in March 2020. The Pennsylvania Department of Environmental Protection revoked PGE's permit to inject waste, citing the township's home-rule charter as grounds for its decision. PGE immediately filed an appeal, and on December 15, 2020, PGE sued Grant Township in federal court (for a second time) to overturn the community's law banning frack waste injection wells. The company was on the defensive and residents rejoiced. "I am hopeful that the haters and naysayers will take note, and that communities will be inspired with what's just happened and run with it," an ecstatic Long told the press. "Fights like ours should mushroom all around Pennsylvania."

* * *

What are rights anyway? We invoke them all the time, but they are not easy to define and rarely if ever absolute, as anyone who has spent time pent up in a "free speech pen" at a protest knows too well. A right is not "some strange substance that one either has or has not," Stone points out in *Trees*. "One's life, one's right to vote, one's property, can all be taken away. But those who would infringe on them must go through certain procedures to do so; these procedures are a measure of what we value in society." The right to remain silent or to bear arms is as irrelevant to a chimpanzee as it is to a human infant, but the latter still has certain inalienable rights, and the former could use some. One former Supreme Court justice described rights as "trump cards." Of course, that doesn't mean government, corporations, and private citizens can't or won't violate them routinely—we know they will. But few of us who feel our rights are imperfectly conceived or protected would give them up.

That we think of rights as something we individually possess is arguably part of their fundamental weakness. That was the position of Karl Marx, who in 1843 wrote,

> None of the so-called rights of man, therefore, go beyond egoistic man, beyond man as a member of civil society— that is, an individual withdrawn into himself, into the confines of his private interests and private caprice, and separated from the community. In the rights of man, he is far from being conceived as a species-being; on the contrary, species-life itself, society, appears as a framework external to the individuals, as a restriction of their original independence. The sole bond holding them together is natural necessity, need and private interest, the preservation of their property and their egoistic selves.

The last thing we need is to further privatize our world by granting plants and animals egoistic fiefdoms. But that is not what the expansion of rights to nonhuman life has to mean, proponents say. Ecosystems are too complex for natural rights to mean that no tree could ever be felled. Instead, CELDF's Nicholson insists, giving rights to nature provides a way to push back on self-interested, acquisitive personhood, opening legal space for humans to recognize themselves as part of the environment, not separate from it, while providing a way to argue that the environment, as a rights-holder, has a value that is not purely economic. Under this framework, a creek or a forest in a poor, rural area has grounds to refuse being sacrificed to private profit, even if its health and thriving provide no immediate measurable financial benefit to humans living nearby.

There is also, always, the question of where rights come from. The 2016 Republican Party platform stipulated "that man-made law must be consistent with God-given, natural rights." The God the drafters refer to is one widely believed to have given humankind dominion over the natural world, not one who would deign to give the natural world rights. To give rights to oceans or octopuses, then, would be to privilege— quite reasonably!—actually existing life over the alleged dictates of an imaginary and typically wrathful man in the sky, and it would also be an affront to the "natural right" to property that is a cornerstone of capitalism.

The citizens of Grant Township, meanwhile, seized new privileges for themselves, whether God intended them or not. In early 2016 they took the dramatic step of legalizing civil disobedience undertaken to prevent the injection well. "Any natural person may . . . enforce the rights and prohibitions of the charter through direct action," the ordinance states. Challenging the legitimacy of the system that completely dismissed them by legalizing resistance to what they believe are unjust laws "was a warning shot, a shot over the bow," Long said. "If the judge says something we don't like, we are not going away." The environment, however, will never be able to seize rights or ask politely for them, which means human allies will have to do that work, however fraught it may be.

* * *

The Little Mahoning Watershed is not the first natural habitat to seek legal rights or redress. With guidance from CELDF, the rights of nature were included in Ecuador's 2008 constitution, and cited to halt two industrial projects. A former national park in New Zealand became a person in the eyes of the law in 2014, and the Whanganui River was granted the same exceptional status in 2017, with Mount Taranaki—a 120,000-year-old stratovolcano—following suit in 2018. All three sites are sacred to the Maori. In 2019, voters in Toledo, Ohio, granted the Lake Erie river watershed personhood rights by an overwhelming 61 to 39 percent, with the aim of protecting the 9,940-square-mile body of water from toxic runoff. Over the years, a variety of cases naming environments and animals as plaintiffs have come before US courts, mainly in response to the Endangered Species Act. *Byram River v. Village of Port Chester*, *Loggerhead Turtle v. County Council of Volusia*, and *Coho Salmon v. Pacific Lumber Company* have all raised the issue of nonhuman personhood and legal standing, though none have had unequivocal success on that particular front. All these cases used additional human coplaintiffs, which lawyers typically include as a kind of insurance that a claim will be heard. In these proceedings, asserting the rights of trees blurs into asserting the rights of ecosystems blurs into asserting the rights of species blurs into asserting the rights of individual nonhuman animals.

While "animal rights" may be a common enough refrain in our culture, those who invoke the phrase rarely mean it. What they are actually referring to is animal welfare, because they are against unnecessary cruelty. Even the philosopher Peter Singer, who is known as the "godfather of animal rights" and author of the 1975 classic *Animal Liberation*, does not put rights for nonhuman creatures front and center—as a utilitarian, his emphasis is on reducing suffering. Likewise, the statutes protecting animals today, including the Animal Welfare Act and the Endangered Species Act, regulate the use and abuse of animals but do not challenge their fundamental legal status.

In contrast to the welfarists, Steven Wise, founder of the Nonhuman Rights Project, has spent thirty years building the legal argument that some nonhuman animals—great apes such as chimpanzees, bonobos, orangutans, and gorillas, as well as dolphins, orcas, belugas, and elephants—should be granted legal personhood on account of their advanced cognitive abilities. "Legal personhood," he writes in his book *Rattling the Cage*, "is the frame upon which we stretch fundamental immunities that block abuses of power, whether that power is rooted in precedent, policy, principle, or prejudice." While Wise relies on detailed affidavits provided by scientists and researchers to make his case that these species possess self-awareness and autonomy, the idea of exceptional animal intelligence is hardly a stretch for laypeople these days thanks to social media. Our digital portals teem with videos of crows solving complex puzzles and dogs breaking out of cages. But as much as we might enjoy procrastinating by gawking at animal ingenuity, granting nonhuman agents the status of "legal persons" with a baseline array of rights remains a major stretch. And though few among us would describe crows or dogs, gorillas or elephants as *things*, that's what they remain according to the law.

Wise's approach tries to provide an answer to a paradox: How can a legal thing sue to challenge its thinghood? Wise eventually found inspiration by looking back at the history of slavery, specifically the famous *Somerset v. Stewart* case. James Somerset, a Black enslaved person purchased in Virginia, accompanied his owner, Charles Stewart, on a journey to England, where slavery was less entrenched than in the United States. Somerset tried to escape but was captured and returned to his owner; as property, he could not sue for his release. In 1772 the English abolitionist Granville Sharp, serving as a legal proxy, filed a writ of habeas corpus in his stead, which the justice, Lord Mansfield, upheld against the commercial interests of slaveholders. A precedent was set as a man who was formerly property became a free person. (Britain abolished the slave trade in 1807 and gave all enslaved people in the empire their freedom in 1833.)

Unlocking the Cage, a documentary directed by Chris Hegedus and D. A. Pennebaker, follows the Nonhuman Rights Project team on its quest to inch forward the march toward nonhuman personhood by suing on behalf of three chimpanzees—Tommy, Leo, and Hercules—to gain their freedom. Tommy was kept in a small enclosure on a property in upstate New York, Leo and Hercules in a laboratory at the State University of New York, Stony Brook. With cameras rolling, Wise passionately makes his case in numerous courtrooms; one judge refuses to entertain the controversial analogy between slavery and animal oppression, advising him to move on to other lines of reasoning, while others appear more open-minded. Wise understands that the law does not progress in a straightforward or linear fashion—it advances and regresses. Judges disagree, then agree, then disagree again. Legal precedents are vague or conflicting. His goal is to create the first small fissures in the legal wall that deems animals worthy of welfare but not rights; it will be up to others to keep chipping away until the barrier disappears.

* * *

Propounding the rights of nature raises countless philosophical and practical riddles. Should invasive species have equal protections? What about the rights of prey against predators? Where does a watershed end if all ecosystems are interconnected? To the common question of whether rights for nature require some kind of corresponding duties, the standard answer is no; after all, human children and some mentally disabled people have rights without responsibilities. While corporate persons can be prosecuted for crimes, a tree that falls on someone's home should not be liable. No need to revive the tradition, routine in the Middle Ages, of bringing animals accused of crimes to trial and punishing them by torture and death. (Some were granted clemency on the basis of their good character—an eighteenth-century French female donkey, embroiled in a bestiality case, was acquitted when prominent members of the community signed a certificate testifying that she was known to be virtuous and "in all her habits of life a most honest creature.") But more unsettling questions remain: How do human advocates know what is best for the rights-holders they aim to help? In *Trees*, for example, Stone recounts a case in which the rights of two dolphins were asserted after a lab assistant liberated them from their tanks into the Pacific Ocean. On being charged for theft (the dolphins were lab property), the assistant countered that he was saving two jural "persons" from slavery. Unfortunately, marine biologists testified that the captivity-bred dolphins would not last long in the wild. The assistant got six months in jail, and the dolphins were never seen again.

What Stone, Wise, and CELDF's Nicholson all maintain is that, however many absurd scenarios one can imagine arising from giving nature rights, the current system is already preposterous in ways nonlawyers don't realize. To improve their chances of winning, environmental lawyers are often forced to frame their arguments around far-fetched injuries or financial inconveniences to humans—the diminishment of property values or reduced business revenue. Likewise, only humans are eligible to be compensated for damages, not ecosystems in need of restoration. The environment is an afterthought of indirect importance as lost profits, an externality subject to a cost-benefit analysis. Cases of habitat destruction or animal abuse have been filed in terms of tragically limiting a human plaintiff's "aesthetic enjoyment" or annoyingly impinging on future vacation plans. A 2008 suit to stop the Navy from killing whales included testimony from tourists about the fulfilling "opportunity to observe and interact with marine species" and the bottomless disappointment they felt knowing they wouldn't be able to "see whales spout as often." The direct harm to whales, beings invisible in the eye of the law, had to be tiptoed around—and the real grievances advocates sought to remedy left unstated because the actual victims lack rights.

For now, those who resist such legal contortions are frequently ridiculed. Long told me that the gas company mocked the people of Grant Township for imparting rights to the environment ("What are you going to do," company officials said, "take a jar of creek water and put it on the stand and have it testify?") while also taking the threat seriously enough to sue. Wise and his team, too, have encountered their fair share of scorn, and Stone's treatise inspired other scholars to reply in jeering verse (*Our brooks will babble in the courts / Seeking damages for torts*). It is true that their efforts seem quixotic at first blush, whimsical or absurd or offensive, but over the last three decades, their arguments have made measurable headway. We have been through revolutions of rights before, they remind us: enslaved people, free Black citizens, Indigenous people, women, children, people with disabilities, and refugees have all had to fight for basic recognition as members of the rights-holding community. Why should we assume that we live at the end of history and all entities worthy of rights or legal personhood have already been identified?

15

OUT OF TIME

Twelve years, or so the scientists told us in 2018. That's how long we had to pull back from the brink of climate catastrophe by constraining global warming to a maximum of 1.5 degrees Celsius. Twelve years to prevent the annihilation of coral reefs, greater melting of the permafrost, and species apocalypse, along with the most dire consequences for human civilization as we know it. Food shortages, forest fires, droughts and monsoons, intensified war and conflict, billions of refugees—we have barely begun to conceive of the range of dystopian futures looming on the horizon. Twelve years, and now we don't even have that. Eleven, ten, nigh, eight.

One person who looks squarely and prophetically at the potential ramifications of climate change and insists on a response is Greta Thunberg, the teenaged environmentalist who launched a global wave of youth climate strikes from her home in Sweden. In April 2019, at the age of sixteen, she gave a tour de force address in the British Parliament, invoking not just her peers who were regularly missing class to protest

---

* Previously published as "Out of Time: Listening to the Climate's Clock," *Lapham's Quarterly* 12, no. 4 (Fall 2019).

government inaction but also those yet to be born. "I speak on behalf of future generations," Thunberg said. "Many of you appear concerned that we are wasting valuable lesson time, but I assure you we will go back to school the moment you start listening to science and give us a future."

Thunberg accepts what many influential adults seem unable to face: the inevitability of change. Change is coming, either in the form of adaptation or annihilation; we can respond proactively or reactively to this discomfiting fact. Perhaps her youth gives her perspective. Twelve years, a little over a decade, is the time for a human infant to become a preteen and for a preteen to become a young adult. For a sixteen-year-old, twelve years is three-fourths of their life, a veritable expanse that, projected forward, will involve crossing the threshold from adolescence to the first stage of maturity. It's ample time to adapt and evolve. Yet for a relatively contented middle-aged or elderly adult, twelve years isn't as substantial—not quite the blink of an eye but a continuation of the present. At a certain point, stasis is the goal, to ward off decline. But decline awaits us all—as the economist John Maynard Keynes bluntly put it, "In the long run we are all dead." Everyone's time on earth must come to an end. The question is, What do we do with such knowledge?

It would be interesting to know what Keynes, vanquisher of financial depressions, would say if he were around to reflect on our present predicament. In his 1930 essay "Economic Possibilities for Our Grandchildren," he optimistically predicted that increasing productivity and boundless growth would usher in an age of shared leisure and abundance. How could he have foreseen that a commitment to never-ending economic expansion would instead yield conditions of massive inequality and ecological instability? Obliviously compelling the extraction of natural resources to meet escalating targets, capitalism inevitably leads to environmental catastrophe. And so we teeter on a precipice.

Faced with the deleterious effects of capitalism's ecologically extractive embrace, a growing number of activists correctly insist that the first step is to dramatically curtail fossil-fuel extraction and emissions and invest in renewable-energy technology, two central pillars of what is now called a Green New Deal. Keeping resources in the ground would mean energy companies forfeiting approximately $20 trillion in assets, a prospect conventional business models will never willingly entertain; those assets are already on the books, factored into future projections, and to abandon them would cause stocks to tumble. At the same time, a just transition to a carbon-neutral society will require trillions of dollars of investment and state action on an unprecedented scale. The moment calls for a radical transformation of the dominant economic calculus, a rejection of its limited conception of value and insatiable appetite for immediate returns. But even mitigating potential damage will demand significant losses for the private sector and colossal public expenditure.

The struggle ahead—and it will be an epic one—will be over who will pay for this transition and when. The science is unequivocal: we must act now because we failed to act decades ago. Meanwhile, the world's plutocrats prefer to procrastinate or block progress, unmoved by the argument that because their past actions disproportionately precipitated the current emergency, they are responsible for repairing and preventing further harm. Some are resistant to reckoning with the full extent of the climate crisis because they are positioned to profit from it. Others are able to buy time by investing in secluded retreats and armed bunkers, hedging bets and speculating on what property will best guarantee their individual security and survival.

For the working class, already stretched thin, time is a luxury fewer and fewer can afford. That was the message of France's Gilets Jaunes, or Yellow Vests, revolt, which erupted in late 2018 in response to an environmentally minded but regressive fuel tax that would have taken the biggest toll on low-income and rural people. In France as elsewhere, expanding prosperity is not evenly shared, with the affluent capturing the bulk of the economic rewards while the less privileged bear the brunt of the ecological crisis, including during a heat wave that claimed several lives in July 2019. Tired of condescending leaders comfortably ensconced in urban centers, aggrieved citizens took to the streets, rallying under a stark slogan: "The elites talk about the *end of the world* while we are talking about the *end of the month*." But some Yellow Vest demonstrators soon adopted a different and more hopeful motto: "End of the world, end of the month, same struggle."

* * *

"For fuck's sake, life expectancy is declining in America," Chloe Watlington laments in a moving essay for *Commune* magazine about the alienation and despair of trying to survive in a winner-take-all society. Rich people are living longer and dreaming of life-extension therapies, but the poor are losing ground, perishing ten to fifteen years earlier on average than their wealthier counterparts. "On a dying planet we are dying sooner. It's like being in an otherwise quiet room with the loud ticking of a nearby clock. Can't you hear it?"

One clock ticks forebodingly. And then another. And another. Mussels are roasting in their shells on the California coast, a mother orca carries her dead calf for seventeen days while her pod goes hungry, clear-cutting quickens pace in the rain forests of Brazil, the Maldives are sinking, and Arctic ice is receding. No wonder we are on edge, with all these alarms perpetually blaring.

Part of the difficulty of addressing the climate crisis has to do with different timescales operating simultaneously. End of the world, end of the month. There are so many clocks and so little time: economic clocks, physical and chemical clocks, nature's innumerable biological clocks, our inner psychological clocks, and collective cultural clocks. It's a temporal cacophony, a disorienting polyrhythm. To figure out how to move forward, we should pause and delineate the different tempos we dwell within.

Capitalism's clock ticks loudest in our ear, setting the primary rhythm we now march to—possibly off a cliff—yet the clock of industrial standardized time is a relatively new phenomenon in human history. For most of our species' existence time was a local affair, noon established by the sun's place in the sky, a fluid movement from east to west. It was not something set by the clearly delineated time zones we now inhabit. *O'clock* is a contraction for *of the clock*, a vestigial reminder that there was a time when clocks were novelties and clock time obviously foreign, an interloper not yet internalized as the societal default.

For eons sun and seasons determined our ancestors' habits. When night fell, work ceased. The first light signaled it was time to begin again. A shadowy sky could make the exact time of day difficult to discern. Industrialization changed that.

As new modes of manufacturing developed, time itself was systematized and commodified. Abstract, regimented modes of measurement eclipsed other ways of conceiving and communicating duration, the impromptu and sporadic yielded to the regularly scheduled and predictably recurrent. In his essay "Time, Work-Discipline, and Industrial Capitalism," the British historian E. P. Thompson invokes Madagascar, where time was measured by "a rice cooking" (about half an hour) or "the frying of a locust" (a moment), and tells of some native communities that spoke of how a "man died in less than the time in which maize is not yet completely roasted" (less than fifteen minutes). As industrialization progressed, all manner of clocks proliferated, a symbol of a new market-driven organization of time and synchronization of labor. Today your clock may be analog or digital, or maybe your clock is your phone. Time may be told by swinging pendulums, the frequency of quartz (32,768 Hz), or via cell-tower link to the vibrations of far-off strontium atoms.

Undergirding this shift in perception and organization was a transformation in energy supply: the shift to fossil fuels. Scattered energy resources—wood, human and animal labor, water, and wind—are no match for coal. Coal turned water into steam, and steam power led to the development of trains, which crisscrossed the country and then the world. Coal seams are the accumulation of past energy reserves, and the discovery of this ecological endowment catalyzed an extractive frenzy. "In the abstract, mankind entered into the possession of a capital inheritance more splendid than all the wealth of the Indies," the inimitable critic Lewis Mumford wrote in *Technics and Civilization* in 1934. But like "a drunken heir on a spree," industrialists began burning through humanity's be-quest. "The psychological results of carboniferous capitalism—the lowered morale, the expectation of getting something for nothing, the disregard for a balanced mode of production and consumption, the habituation to wreckage and debris as part of the normal human environment—all of these results were plainly mischievous." Out of this mischief "carboniferous capitalism" was born. Coal, gas, and oil allowed for the accumulation of power in a triple sense—mechanical power, social power, and economic power—by the few who controlled the sources and supply chains.

This is the moment we leaped into the unknown. The dawn of carboniferous capitalism marked the beginning of what scientists, in a 1957 paper, called "a large-scale geophysical experiment of a kind that could not have happened in the past nor be reproduced in the future." The industrial revolution set into motion a chain of events that would begin to reverse protracted natural processes at breakneck speed: "Within a few centuries we are returning to the atmosphere and oceans the concentrated organic carbon stored in sedimentary rocks over hundreds of millions of years."

Carbon has its own clock, the cadence of physical and chemical laws and facts of prehistory offering a counterbeat to modern capitalism, which seeks short-term gains and predictable outcomes pegged to a calendar. Fossil fuels, in contrast, are the past condensed, and the physical processes unleashed through their consumption are not linear, which is why scientists warn of "tipping points." Every barrel of oil represents both a swath of land and an epoch of life—the product of photosynthesis and the geological remains of once-living organisms—concentrated to its potent essence. Two and a half centuries after the industrial revolution began, we are finally forced to come to grips with the consequences of burning coal. The coal put to work in nineteenth-century Manchester shapes our environment today, just as the emissions from the burning of fuels from Saudi oil fields, US natural gas reserves, and Canadian tar sands will haunt life on earth for a long time to come. "Global warming is a sun mercilessly projecting a new light onto history," writes Andreas Malm in *Fossil Capital*, a history of steam power. "If we wait some time longer and then demolish the fossil economy in one giant blow, it would still cast a shadow far into the future: emissions slashed to zero, the sea might continue to rise for many hundreds of years." By burning up the past, we imperil everything to come.

We can see the danger in the environment around us. Nature's timekeeping methods are increasingly confused. Delicately evolved biological clocks erratically speed up or slow down. In some places, flowers and leaves bud too early, with devastating results. In 1751 the botanist and taxonomist Carl Linnaeus proposed a *horologium florae*, or flower clock, a hypothetical garden that would allow a fanciful form of tracking the hours based on the fact that certain plants bloom at certain times of day. Linnaeus's flower clock was never really going to catch on, because as Ziya Tong explains in her revelatory book *The Reality Bubble*, the time when many flowers open depends not just on a particular hour but also on the amount of available daylight. The timekeeping would be hyperlocal and at the whim of the weather, not dissimilar to a sundial rendered useless by cloud cover. But with climate change, Tong warns, such flower clocks "have begun to bloom at unusual times"—off not just by hours or days but weeks or even months.

While hardly suitable for maintaining a tight work schedule, *horologia florae* exist on a more fundamental level. Plants blossom and fade at specific times during the year, and creatures are dependent on their cycles, a complex dance involving plants, pollinators, and other animals. Tong reports that in 2016, over six hundred plant species bloomed early, according to a study by the Botanical Society of Britain and Ireland. Plants and animals are increasingly out of sync with each other, something experts in phenology—the study of the timing of biological events such as plants flowering and insects laying eggs—call a "mismatch." Biologists who pay attention to natural physiological rhythms and cyclical and seasonal phenomena have begun to notice that the interaction between species is shifting off the beat.

Desynchronization upsets delicate relationships between migration, reproduction, and survival with cascading consequences. Not all species use the same temporal cues. A growing number of birds now arrive late for spring, having timed their migration with the sun, while many plants are more attuned to changes in temperature. A warming climate can mean leaves shoot early, encouraging insects to emerge to feast, but by the time migrating birds arrive to eat the insects, they are already gone. Flowers may bloom before—or sometimes after—pollinating beetles, bees, or wasps appear, symbiotic partners out of step to the detriment of both. Other dependent but increasingly off-rhythm pairs abound: spider orchids and mining bees, puffins and herring, caribou and lichen, the red admiral butterfly and the stinging nettle. "Oak tree buds are eaten by winter moths, whose caterpillars are in turn fed by great tits to their chicks, but the synchronicity of all these events has been disrupted," the *Guardian* observed. One scientist explained, "There will be progressive disruption of pollination systems with climatic warming, which could lead to the breakdown of co-evolved interactions between species."

The shortsighted actions of one species are the source of the mismatch—our species. We are out of sync with everything on earth and even with one another. There are 7.7 billion human beings and counting, each of us possessing a kind of inner clock, a unique expression of lived time. For *Homo sapiens*, time is strange not only because it is relative, as Albert Einstein and others revealed, but because it is subjective; it is not only biological, like the clocks of flowers and trees, but also psychological. Our personal experiences of time are inconsistent, mutable. In childhood a month can linger for an eternity. For someone in middle age, a season unspools at a disorienting clip.

Sometimes time can slow. Both boredom and awe make the seconds stretch, and so does fear, an emotion likely to be evoked if you read the latest climate news. The problem is that fear does not provoke rational action to address the urgent problem at hand. While a subset of committed activists and hardline survivalists are motivated by grim statistics and respond productively to warnings about rising CO_2 levels, research shows that doom-and-gloom messaging doesn't work across the board. "Apocalyptic rhetoric causes most people to just ignore it," Joanna Huxster, a professor of environmental studies at Eckerd College, told me. "It creates a shutdown."

Huxster and other academics interested in science communication are trying to figure out what makes us tick: Which messages facilitate constructive action and which provoke apathy, panic, anger, or denial? Time plays a role in marking the difference. You can see the challenge, she explained, in the fact that we don't naturally distinguish between weather and climate, though they are distinct phenomena. Huxster tells her students that climate is how you choose your vacation site, weather is how you know what to pack. Climate unfolds on a grand scale that is difficult to perceive, shifting over years, decades, centuries, or millennia. Weather, in contrast, is immediate and imminent, captured in a ten-day forecast.

Part of the problem is that most of us have difficulty conceiving of the past and the future. Our weather memories are unreliable. We project the present onto the past, assuming that summers were always as roasting or winters as snowless as they are now. At the same time, we struggle to imagine a few decades ahead. The years 2100 or 2050—dates widely discussed in climate research—are simply too far away to feel acute for most people. Human-centered messaging that is now or near-term and focused on fairness (rather than the nuances of scientific research) are most effective, research shows. This is the small upside to climate scientists' recent determination that their earlier projections were too optimistic and that we must act swiftly. Twelve years is a "graspable amount of time," according to Huxster—short enough so that it is difficult (though still not impossible) to ignore the sound of the clock.

* * *

Part of the anxiety many of us feel around climate change is the fact that no one knows what will happen next. But perhaps that's the wrong way to think about it. The ancient Greek root *chronos* means chronological time, a sequential unfolding. But the ancient Greeks complemented it with *kairos*, which meant a propitious moment, the time for decision or action—a term that in modern Greek has coincidentally come to mean weather. Perhaps the opportune time to intervene is fleeting, like a passing thunderstorm or the peak of spring, and we risk a mismatch by striking too late.

Which brings us back to the striking children, the teenagers in revolt. They understand what time it is: it is time to act. Young people around the world are angry, because they feel their futures have been stolen and sold, along with those of generations to come. Capitalist mantras of endless economic growth and intensifying extraction rationalize a kind of trans-temporal theft, a ransacking of both collective patrimony (the planet's accumulated bounty) and prospects (its continuing habitability). Perhaps it makes sense that children, who usually are closer to birth than death, would relate strongly to people who have not yet been born and defend their interests.

"Man is born a debtor to society," the French statesman Léon Bourgeois wrote in 1895. From first breath, each of us is bound in a complex web of relationships that transcend the current moment. Thinking of time as chronological might be part of what is holding us back from finding a sustainable path. Past, present, future—climate change combines all these registers at once. Time is not an arrow, relentlessly moving forward, but something circular and strange, to quote the Potawatomi botanist Robin Wall Kimmerer, more akin to "a lake in which the past, present, and future exist," than a rushing river. We need a new vocabulary and new understandings—or maybe we need to revive concepts and traditions unjustly deemed relics of an outmoded, obsolete age by a dominant culture invested in their disappearance.

When he was twenty-seven, Tł'akwasik'an Khelsilem founded Kwi Awt Stelmexw, an arts and culture organization in Vancouver that offers language classes. Only one original Skwxwú7mesh (often called Squamish) language speaker remains, but that person is now part of a broader community of around fifty speakers and learners that is steadily expanding, in good part due to Khelsilem's efforts. A linguist, activist, and philosopher, and a Skwxwú7mesh Nation council member, Khelsilem explained that the phrase *Kwi Awt Stelmexw* does not easily translate into English but can be interpreted as both "the last people" and "the coming after people," both ancestors and descendants. The people of the past and future, while not exactly one entity, are also not opposed. "*Awt* refers to something that comes after or first, which is confusing," he told me. There is both a temporal and spatial component to the term. "One way to think about this is the ones that are coming after you— which sounds like they are behind us instead of in front of us. They are behind us and yet ahead." The people coming behind us in space are also the people who are ahead of us in time.

The challenge, Khelsilem said, is how to thread the needle between "the ideological battle between endless progress and great nostalgia," a phrase he attributes to another local Vancouver organizer, Matt Hern. Given the history of colonization—a kind of apocalypse in itself—Indigenous communities have a unique perspective on the promise of both past and future, on tradition and what will happen next. "A central belief is that the quality of life we had before colonization was much better than we have now. There is an urge to restore. There is something that we are trying to revitalize, because it has the possibility to improve the lives of our people," Khelsilem told me, explaining why language reclamation is so important. "It's a structure of looking at the work of predecessors and seeing that we need to pay it forward, and wanting to make a life for those living now and those who will be. It comes from a place of a lot of gratitude."

Gratitude toward those who came before necessitates taking care of those who exist now or one day will. The present is a spoke, linking us forward and backward in time through bonds of affection, obligation, innovation, and possibility.

In contrast, capitalist settler-colonial culture imagines the present as little more than a pit stop on the superhighway to a better tomorrow, a truncated outlook that allows us to imagine ourselves as the primary beneficiaries of progress. A better tomorrow, we might be around to see. A better next century or two would be aimed at others, at posterity.

Where has this attitude gotten us? The destination remains unknown, but we've hit a fork in the road: shift course or race off the cliff, taking the striking children's futures down with us. As we burn through our common ecological inheritance at the behest of an intransigent economic elite, the past haunts the present, transforming natural cycles and looming ominously over everything to come. To survive the burgeoning climate crisis, we need to reckon with our relationship to time. The seeds of approaches that might help ensure sustainability and survival may have been sown long ago; in our quest for solutions, we should look to long-standing principles and not only pray for a quick technological fix. The ancient recognition of time's polyrhythmic and sometimes staccato unfolding, with an ear tuned to *kairotic* rupture and a more expansive notion of solidarity across generations, may be just what this moment calls for. "End of the world, end of the month, same struggle"— the slogan speaks a profound truth, but we still must work to make it real. Somehow we have to manage to conceive of multiple timescales and horizons at once, or we are toast.

ACKNOWLEDGMENTS

Special thanks to the various editors who worked on these essays. Christopher Frey edited "Failing Better" for *Hazlitt*. I'm grateful to John Summers for bringing me into the *Baffler* magazine's orbit, where I worked with the talented Lucie Elvin on "Against Activism," "Who Speaks for the Trees?," and "Our Friends Who Live across the Sea." The inimitable prose-stylist Chris Lehmann edited "Who, the People?" and "The Dads of Tech" at the *Baffler* before he moved on to the *New Republic*, where he commissioned "Reclaiming the Future." The *New Republic* also published "The End of the University," under the insightful guidance of Emily Cooke. At the *New Yorker* I worked with Joshua Rothman and Carla Blumenkranz on "The Right to Listen" and "Wipe the Slate Clean," respectively—both pushed me to think more rigorously and express myself more clearly. Max Strasser at the *New York Times* had the idea for "Out With the Old," and helped make the piece what it is. It's always a pleasure to work with Ben Tarnoff, who edited both "The Automation Charade" and "The Insecurity Machine" for *Logic Magazine*. I was lucky to collaborate with the wonderful Sarah Fan on "Out of Time" for *Lapham's Quarterly*.

It's a huge honor to be published by Haymarket Books, a beacon of radical thought in dark times and a source of good writing for the ages. Enormous thanks to Anthony Arnove, whom I am lucky to call a friend, a comrade, and an editor, and to the rest of the team: Rory Fanning, Charlotte Heltai, and Michael Trudeau, who went above and beyond the call of duty as copyeditor to improve the text. I'm grateful to so many fellow writers who inspire me, especially my dear pal the essayist extraordinaire, Rebecca Solnit. It was huge fun to write "The Dads of Tech" with Joanne McNeil, and I'm thrilled she let me republish it here. Thanks to my amazing sister Nye Taylor for help with the book's cover and the endless moral support and instructions to chill out, and to the extended Taylor gang for kinship and comradery. Boundless love to my partner and best friend, Jeff Mangum, who not only puts up with my obsessions but also encourages and cheers them. I owe a huge thanks to everyone involved with the Debt Collective, the most curious, creative, compassionate, and anticapitalist group of people I know. My final thoughts are with David Graeber, who initially invited me into the debt resistance movement. Just before he passed away, I texted him saying what a "damn good writer" he was, adding that it's a "rare skill among lefties." He replied: "I call it 'being nice to the reader,' which is an extension of the politics, in a sense." Though David's style and insight are hard to match, I've done my best to write with the same generous spirit. He is missed.

INDEX

ABOUT HAYMARKET BOOKS

Haymarket Books is a radical, independent, nonprofit book publisher based in Chicago.

Our mission is to publish books that contribute to struggles for social and economic justice. We strive to make our books a vibrant and organic part of social movements and the education and development of a critical, engaged, international left.

We take inspiration and courage from our namesakes, the Haymarket martyrs, who gave their lives fighting for a better world. Their 1886 struggle for the eight-hour day—which gave us May Day, the international workers' holiday—reminds workers around the world that ordinary people can organize and struggle for their own liberation. These struggles continue today across the globe—struggles against oppression, exploitation, poverty, and war.

Since our founding in 2001, Haymarket Books has published more than five hundred titles. Radically independent, we seek to drive a wedge into the risk-averse world of corporate book publishing. Our authors include Noam Chomsky, Arundhati Roy, Rebecca Solnit, Angela Y. Davis, Howard Zinn, Amy Goodman, Wallace Shawn, Mike Davis, Winona LaDuke, Ilan Pappé, Richard Wolff, Dave Zirin, Keeanga-Yamahtta Taylor, Nick Turse, Dahr Jamail, David Barsamian, Elizabeth Laird, Amira Hass, Mark Steel, Avi Lewis, Naomi Klein, and Neil Davidson. We are also the trade publishers of the acclaimed Historical Materialism Book Series and of Dispatch Books.

ABOUT THE AUTHOR

Astra Taylor is a filmmaker, writer, and political organizer. She is the director of multiple documentaries including *What Is Democracy?* and the author of *Democracy May Not Exist, but We'll Miss It When It's Gone* and the American Book Award–winning *The People's Platform: Taking Back Power and Culture in the Digital Age.* She is cofounder of the Debt Collective, a union for debtors, and contributed the foreword to the group's book, *Can't Pay, Won't Pay: The Case for Economic Disobedience and Debt Abolition.*